Scrap-Basket Sensations

MORE GREAT QUILTS FROM 2½" STRIPS

Kim Brackett

Martingale®
& COMPANY

Dedication
To J.D., the love of my life

Scrap-Basket Sensations:
More Great Quilts from 2½" Strips
© 2011 by Kim Brackett

That Patchwork Place® is an imprint of
Martingale & Company®.

Martingale & Company
19021 120th Ave. NE, Suite 102
Bothell, WA 98011-9511 USA
www.martingale-pub.com

Printed in China
16 15 14 13 12 11   8 7 6 5 4 3

Library of Congress Cataloging-in-Publication Data is available upon request.

ISBN: 978-1-60468-014-0

Mission Statement

Dedicated to providing quality products
and service to inspire creativity.

Credits

President & CEO: Tom Wierzbicki
Editor in Chief: Mary V. Green
Managing Editor: Tina Cook
Technical Editor: Laurie Baker
Copy Editor: Melissa Bryan
Design Director: Stan Green
Production Manager: Regina Girard
Illustrator: Laurel Strand
Cover & Text Designer: Adrienne Smitke
Photographer: Brent Kane

Acknowledgments

Without the help of three very special women, you probably wouldn't be holding this book in your hands. Karen Williamson, Mary Flynn, and Darlene Johannis made many of the sample quilts. They were very generous with their time and extraordinary talent, and I will never be able to thank them adequately.

Thank you to the Warm Company for supplying my favorite batting for the sample quilts. I encourage you to visit their website at www.warmcompany.com to learn all about their fabulous products.

Thank you to the staff of Martingale & Company for so graciously putting up with me and for allowing me the opportunity to do this again. And thank you to Laurie Baker for instinctively knowing what I really meant to say.

Contents

Introduction	4
Tools and Supplies	5
Gathering 2½"-Wide Strips	6
Cutting the Strips	7
Sorting and Storing 2½" Strips	9
Choosing Fabrics for a Project	10
Basic Quiltmaking Instructions	11
Special Piecing Techniques	17
PROJECTS	
Town Square	18
Flowers for Nana Girl	21
Tool Shed	24
Lake Cabin	27
Over and Under	30
Nova	34
Blessings from the Hollow	38
Summer Daze	44
Blues Crossing	47
Scrap-Basket Paddle Wheel	50
Island Chain	53
Tipsy Baskets	56
Sparkler	60
Flower Boxes	63
Bali Breeze	66
Picnic	69
Northern Comfort	72
Twinkle	76
About the Author	79

Introduction

After three dozen quilts, I'm still amazed by the design possibilities for quilts using 2½" strips. Surprisingly, each quilt has been every bit as much fun to make as the first. You would think it would be difficult to imagine different ways to combine simple squares and rectangles, but there are so many possibilities that I won't be able to make them all in my lifetime.

The idea for *Scrap-Basket Surprises* (Martingale & Company, 2009) developed after I had collected an unmanageable amount of scraps. Whenever I began a new quilting project, I rarely considered using the scraps, so they multiplied over the years. After cutting all of them into 2½" strips, I discovered that I'm much more likely to reach for the forgotten treasures to include in my projects. I also discovered that I love mixing some of my older fabrics with precut strips from Moda Jelly Rolls and Hoffman Bali Pops to achieve a much scrappier look.

I hope you'll dig into your scrap basket, throw in some precut strips and stash fabrics, and sew along with me!

Tools and Supplies

Listed in this section are basic materials and supplies used to make the quilts in this book. Some of my personal preferences are indicated, but you may want to experiment with rulers, threads, and tools to determine your own preferences.

Acrylic rotary-cutting rulers: I recommend a 6" x 24" ruler for cutting 2½" strips as well as for cutting longer units for blocks. A large square ruler (12" or larger) is helpful when squaring up blocks and for making the quilt "Scrap-Basket Paddle Wheel" on page 50. A 6½" square ruler with a 45° line is perfect for crosscutting the strips into smaller segments and marking the sewing lines on folded-corner units (see "Folded-Corner Units" on page 17).

Fine-lead mechanical pencil: I prefer this kind of pencil for marking sewing lines on folded-corner units.

Iron and ironing board: A steam iron is helpful when ironing fabric and pressing seam allowances.

Measuring tape: I "borrowed" my husband's metal measuring tape a few years ago. It's very useful for measuring fabric lengths and batting and for measuring quilts when adding borders.

Painter's tape: Use painter's tape for making a temporary sewing guide on your machine for folded-corner units and for preparing the quilt top for basting.

Pins: Use glass-head pins or quilter's pins with a thin shaft.

Rotary cutter and mat: If the blade on your rotary cutter doesn't close automatically, develop the habit of closing it when it's not in use (for your own safety). A sharp blade will make cutting much easier. Use your rotary cutter on a self-healing mat designed for cutting. Keep it clean and free of dust to prolong the life of your rotary-cutter blade.

Seam ripper: Any type of seam ripper will work as long as it's sharp enough to cut the thread without distorting the fabric.

Sewing machine: Have your machine serviced regularly and clean it often according to the manufacturer's instructions.

Sewing-machine needles: I like to use a size 80/12 Sharp or Universal needle for piecing.

Sharp scissors: Use sewing shears for cutting fabric. Keep a small pair of scissors close to your sewing machine for clipping threads.

Spray starch: I use spray starch when ironing fabric to remove wrinkles and for adding body and stability to the fabric before cutting strips.

Thread: Use a high-quality cotton thread for piecing. I like to use tan or gray for piecing scrap quilts. These neutral colors blend well with multiple fabrics.

Walking foot: In addition to being useful for machine quilting, a walking foot is also good for attaching binding to your finished quilt. If your sewing machine didn't come equipped with this attachment, your local sewing-machine dealer can help you find one that will fit your machine.

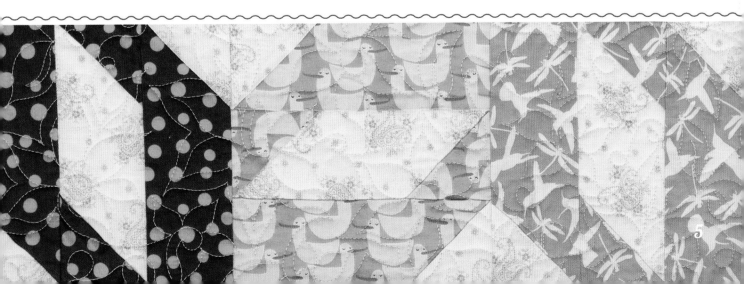

Gathering 2½"-Wide Strips

Each quilt "recipe" in this book contains a list of materials you will need to complete the quilt. The main ingredient in each list is an assortment of 2½"-wide strips. Following are some suggestions to help you build your collection of strips so that most of the cutting will be done before you begin your project.

BEGIN WITH YOUR SCRAP BASKET

If you're a serious quilter, you probably have lots of scraps left over from different projects, purchased in those irresistible grab bags, and given to you by family and friends. Dump your scraps onto a table or the floor and sort them into usable pieces (anything larger than 2½" square). Discard any fabrics that aren't quality 100% cotton. Toss out any loosely woven fabrics that you can see through, as well as any extremely stiff fabrics. If you suspect that a fabric has never been washed, test for colorfastness by thoroughly wetting a small piece and allowing it to dry on a white paper towel. If any color shows on the paper towel after the fabric scrap dries, it will more than likely bleed onto other fabrics in your quilt. At this point, you can either discard the fabric or wash it until you're sure all the excess dye has been removed.

STASH FABRICS

Even before I owned a substantial "stash," I purposely made scrap quilts using as many different fabrics as possible. As a beginning quilter, however, it took time for me to understand that not all fabrics work well together in a scrap quilt. Before this epiphany, some of the strangest fabrics followed me home. I would buy small pieces of anything that caught my eye, whether or not it worked with the palette with which I later became comfortable. As I narrowed down my favorite styles and colors, I overlooked these impulse fabrics when selecting pieces for quilts. You, too, probably own fabrics that beg the question, "What was I thinking?" If so, use these fabrics to build your collection of 2½" strips. I have successfully combined calico fabrics from the 1980s with Civil War–era reproduction fabrics, and plaids with batiks!

PRECUT STRIPS

Some fabric manufacturers offer bundles or rolls of 2½" strips that usually contain a strip from each fabric in a single collection. Using these collections will give your quilt a "designer" look. This is also an economical way to collect a wide variety of strips without having to buy yardage of each piece in a specific line. Precut bundles commonly contain 40 different fabric strips, but some collections are packaged with two strips of each fabric. And because they're precut, most of the work is already done! Some of the quilts in this book require more strips than are in a precut bundle, but if you buy two of them, you can pick and choose your favorite strips for your project and use the leftover strips in another project later.

A bundle and rolls of precut 2½" strips

STRIP CLUBS

A "strip club" isn't what it sounds like! Your local quilt shop may offer a strip-of-the-month club. Customers pay a monthly fee for bundles of strips cut from new fabric bolts as they arrive in the shop. This is a great way to collect a variety of strips in styles and colors that you might not find in your stash.

STRIP SWAPS

Offer to host a swap at your guild meeting. Ask each participant to bring a predetermined number of 2½" strips to swap with others. Be sure that everyone is aware of any guidelines for the swap. The guidelines should at least require that all fabrics are good-quality quilting fabrics. You could also specify themes for certain months, such as Christmas strips for December, pink and red strips for February, and so on.

NEW FABRICS

After you have sorted your 2½" strips and have chosen a project, select all the strips you think will work in that project. If you need more strips, or if you need a larger variety of fabrics for interest, take a trip to your local quilt shop or fabric store. Bring your strips with you, and then buy small amounts (a quarter of a yard) of fabrics that coordinate with the style and colors you already have. Cut these new fabrics into 2½" strips. Use what you need for your project and store the others by style or color for use in future projects. If you're a new quilter, or if you just don't have any scraps, start from scratch and purchase whatever you like to make your quilt.

Cutting the Strips

Accurate cutting is essential for creating a successful quilt. Whether cutting from scraps or from yardage, follow the guidelines in this section to ensure that your strips and other elements of the quilt are cut accurately.

CUTTING FROM SCRAPS

Iron your scraps to remove any wrinkles before cutting. Use spray starch for the more stubborn wrinkles and to add body and stability to the fabrics. You will usually want to cut the longest strip possible. To even up the fabric for cutting, place the fabric scrap on your cutting mat so that the longest edge is vertical. Place your ruler on the fabric scrap near the right edge, following the grain line of the fabric and making sure that any uneven edges extend beyond the ruler. If it's difficult to determine where the grain line is, you may find it helpful to turn the scrap wrong side up, as the threads in the fabric seem more apparent from the wrong side. Cut along the right side of the ruler to trim off the uneven edges. Rotate your cutting mat 180° so that the straightened edge is now on

your left. Place the 2½" mark of the ruler on the straightened edge of the fabric, and then cut along the right side of the ruler.

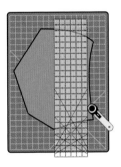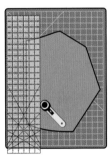

Continue to make cuts in 2½" increments across the fabric. To save time, cut up to four or five scraps at once. Place the largest scraps on the bottom and keep cutting until you run out of fabric. Save the leftover "strings" (pieces narrower than 2½") for making string-pieced quilts at another time.

CUTTING FROM YARDAGE

Because the selvage edges shrink differently than the rest of the fabric, I like to remove these edges before cutting strips. Open the fabric and iron it to remove any wrinkles and to eliminate the original fold line. Fold the fabric in half with what were previously the selvage edges together, placing the folded edge nearest to you. Place a horizontal line toward the bottom edge of your ruler along the fold line. Cut along the right side of the ruler to even the edge of the fabric.

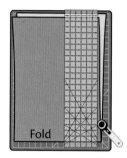

Rotate your cutting mat 180° so that the straightened edge of the fabric is on your left. (If you're cutting from fabric that is longer than your mat, gently fold the excess fabric onto the mat before rotating so that the fabric you just straightened doesn't move from its place on the mat.) Place the 2½" mark of the ruler on the trimmed edge and cut along the right side of the ruler to cut your strip.

Continue to cut in 2½" increments until you have enough strips. **Note**: If you're left-handed, place the ruler on the left of the fabric for the straightening cut, and then rotate the mat so that you cut strips from the right edge of the fabric.

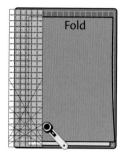

For all other pieces in the quilt that are to be cut from yardage, such as borders and binding strips, follow the preceding instructions using the required measurement.

CROSSCUTTING STRIPS

To cut a strip into smaller segments, trim the selvage edge so that it is straight and squared at a 90° angle. Using a small ruler, place the mark of the desired measurement on the left edge of the strip. Cut along the right side of the ruler. Continue to cut until you have the required number of pieces.

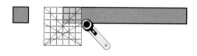

Sorting and Storing 2½" Strips

Initially I tossed all of my precut strips into a large tote bag. It wasn't long before my neatly cut strips turned into a stringy, wrinkled mess with frayed edges. To avoid this, I now fold my strips and stack them neatly in clear plastic storage containers. This allows me to retrieve strips easily, without spending a lot of time searching for certain colors or styles, and it prevents the strips from becoming wrinkled and frayed.

After cutting strips from yardage, fold them in half again so they measure one-quarter the original width of the fabric. Stack them on top of each other with the folded edges facing the same direction. Place two stacks of strips side by side in a *clear* shoebox-sized storage container. These containers stack nicely on shelves and in closets, and because they're transparent, you'll be able to determine at a glance each container's contents. You'll also be able to pick up a stack of strips and locate whatever you need by flipping through the folded ends without disturbing the stacks.

If your strips aren't cut from the full width of fabric (such as pieces cut from your scrap basket), you'll have varying lengths of strips. Just fold these strips until they fit into the storage container. If the strips are fairly short, stack them together and secure them with a bag clip.

Determine how you will sort your strips. If you don't have many strips, you may want to keep all of them in the same container. If you have lots of strips, however, you can use a separate container for each color or style, or perhaps a separate container for each future project. Examples of styles you may have collected could include Christmas fabrics, 1930s reproduction fabrics, homespun plaids, batiks, or bright fabrics. When storing your strips by color, include all fabrics in that color range. For example, store all of your blue strips together, regardless of whether the blues are pastel, grayish, or bright. I try to keep look-alike fabrics together so that I don't have to search through an entire container to find a particular style or shade of blue.

Fold and stack strips to fit in storage container. Clip short strips with a bag clip.

Choosing Fabrics for a Project

If your scrap basket is anything like mine, you'll have fabrics in a wide variety of colors and styles. At this point you could decide to use all of these random fabrics in the same quilt for a really scrappy look, but if you'd like a more coordinated appearance, choose a theme or color scheme for your quilt.

Most of the designs in this book rely on contrast between the main fabrics and the background fabrics. If you choose a project that uses scraps for the background instead of a single fabric, try to use fabrics that blend well together and don't stand apart from each other too much. Otherwise, the overall quilt design could get lost.

THEMES

Theme quilts can be a lot of fun. Just pull out all of your strips that have anything to do with your theme, and then add other fabrics that look like they belong in the quilt. For example, if you have lots of leftover Christmas fabrics from other quilt and craft projects, you could start there. Gather everything that looks like a Christmas print—trees, angels, stars, Santas, gingerbread men, etc. Choose only the fabrics that look good together. Then throw in some "regular" fabrics that blend well with your Christmas fabrics. Other examples of theme quilt fabrics might be autumn-leaf prints, 1930s reproduction prints, Civil War–era reproduction prints, plaids, and batiks.

COLOR SCHEMES

Ideas for color schemes can come from anywhere—just look around. Be alert for color combinations that catch your eye in clothing, magazines, nature, and the quilts of others. Sometimes I like to start with a medium- to large-scale multicolored print for a quilt border, and then select fabrics that match some or all of the colors contained in that print. Some color schemes to consider might be red and white, blue and tan, or pink and green.

If you are fortunate enough to have a flannel or felt design wall in your sewing area, use it to audition strips for your quilt. If you don't have a design wall, you can always make a portable version by using the back of a flannel-backed vinyl tablecloth. Just hang it over a door or tape it to a wall with painter's tape. Stick the main strips (usually darker fabrics) vertically on the design wall next to each other, and then stick on the background strips. Stand back to see if there are any renegades you'd like to eliminate, such as dark fabrics that are too light or fabrics that aren't the right color. When you're pleased with the way the fabrics all look together on the wall, it's time to begin your project!

Basic Quiltmaking Instructions

This section outlines basic skills and techniques necessary for making quilts. Often in quiltmaking, there are many different ways to accomplish the same task. These are the methods that I prefer, but I would suggest that you experiment with other methods to determine which may work best for you and provide more enjoyment as you make your quilt.

YARDAGE REQUIREMENTS

The instructions for the quilts featured in this book assume a 42" usable width of fabric after prewashing and trimming the selvage edges. The cutting instructions indicate the number of 2½" strips required to make the quilts if the strips are cut 2½" across the full width of the fabric. However, many of the quilts were made using a combination of full-width strips, smaller scraps, and stash fabrics, so the cutting instructions also include a separate listing with the total number of pieces to cut if you're using scraps or a combination of scraps and strips. Please note that the "Cutting from Scraps" box included with each project's instructions contains the number of pieces to cut for the body of the quilt only. You will still need to follow the "Cutting" instructions for cutting other pieces such as the borders and binding.

MACHINE PIECING

Whether or not you adhere to any of the quiltmaking "rules" you've learned, you should always try to achieve an accurate ¼" seam allowance. If your seam allowance is too wide or too narrow, the measurement of your blocks will not be accurate, thereby causing your quilt to be warped and uneven. For accurate piecing, use a ¼" presser foot if your machine is equipped with one. If not, your local sewing-machine dealer can help you find one that will work with your machine. In the meantime, you can make your own temporary ¼" seam guide by using a piece of painter's tape or the sticky edge of a sticky note. Place the tape ¼" to the right of your needle for a sewing guide, making sure that the tape doesn't touch your feed dogs.

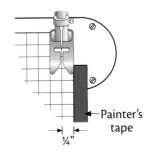

Painter's tape

¼"

To test the accuracy of your seam allowance, sew together three rectangles, 2½" x 6½", as shown. The measurement of the middle strip should be exactly 2" wide. The measurement from the left edge to the right edge should be 6½" and the block should be 6½" square. If your test sample does not measure exactly as shown in the illustration, you will need to adjust your seam allowance appropriately.

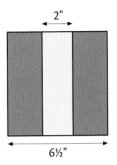

2"

6½"

CHAIN PIECING

Whenever possible, chain piece pairs of units together to make the most economical use of your time and your thread. Sew a pair of pieces together, sewing a couple of stitches beyond the edge. Without cutting the thread and without moving the first pair of pieces, begin sewing the next pair. Continue to sew in this manner until all of your pairs are sewn. Remove your "chain" of pieces from the machine and clip the threads at the end. Clip carefully between each pair of sewn pieces.

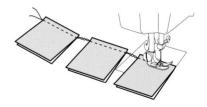

PRESSING

To press seam allowances after sewing, lay the unit on your ironing board without opening it. Press the sewn seam flat by moving your iron in an up-and-down motion. Open the unit and press the seam allowances in the desired direction.

The project instructions indicate the direction to press seam allowances. Illustrations are provided as well, with the pressing direction indicated by arrows. If it doesn't matter which way the seam allowances are pressed, the instructions will direct you to "press the seam allowances in either direction."

To reduce bulk where multiple seam allowances meet, I like to press the seam allowances in a clockwise or counterclockwise direction. Using a seam ripper, remove the stitching above the horizontal seam allowance as shown in the photograph below. From the back of the block, use your thumbs and forefingers to finger-press the seam allowances in the direction indicated. Turn the block over and press from the front with an iron.

Remove stitching.

Finger-press in a clockwise or counterclockwise direction.

ADDING BORDERS

Adding borders to your quilts serves multiple purposes. Plain borders can stop the chaos in the center of a busy quilt by providing a visual resting place. They also add extra width and length to your quilt without the necessity of piecing extra blocks. Pieced borders can add an interesting design element to the outside edges of your quilt. Whatever your intent may be for adding borders, take time to measure to ensure a successful outcome.

Butted-Corner Borders

1. Smooth out your pieced quilt top as flat as possible. Measure the length of the quilt top through the center. Use this measurement to cut border strips for both sides of the quilt top, piecing the strips as necessary. Mark the center along the side edges of the quilt top and mark the center of the border strips along one long edge using a pencil. Pin the border strips, right sides together, to the side edges of the quilt top at the center marks and the ends. Finish pinning the border strips in place. Sew the side-border strips to the quilt top and press the seam allowances toward the borders unless otherwise indicated.

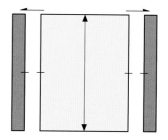

Measure center of quilt, top to bottom. Mark centers.

2. Measure the width of the quilt top, including the side borders. Use this measurement to cut borders for the top and bottom edges of the quilt top. Piece the border strips if necessary. Mark the center of the top and bottom edges of the quilt top and mark the center of the border strips along one long side using a pencil. Pin the border strips, right sides together, to the top and bottom edges of the quilt top at the center marks and the ends. Finish pinning the border strips in place. Sew the top- and bottom-border strips

to the quilt top, and press the seam allowances toward the borders unless otherwise indicated.

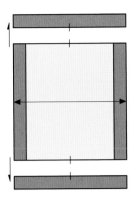

Measure center of quilt, side to side, including border strips. Mark centers.

3. Repeat steps 1 and 2 if your quilt has multiple butted-corner borders.

Mitered-Corner Borders

Mitered corners can be used to achieve amazing visual effects when using directional fabrics, special border prints, and striped fabrics. The design meets precisely at the corners and seems to encircle the quilt. When adding multiple borders, sew the border strips together first, and then cut the border in one piece as you would for a single border.

1. Measure the length of the quilt top. Multiply the width of the cut border strip by 2 and add that number to the measurement of your quilt top. Add about 4" to this measurement just to be sure your strips will be long enough for the mitered corner. (It's much easier to trim than to add!)

SIDE-BORDER STRIPS

Unfinished length of quilt top: _____
Add: Width of cut border strips x 2: _____
Add: _____ 4"

....

Length to cut side-border strips: _____

2. Measure the width of the quilt top. Multiply the width of the cut border strip by 2 and add that number to the measurement of your quilt top. Add about 4" to this measurement just to be sure your strips will be long enough for the mitered corner.

TOP- AND BOTTOM-BORDER STRIPS

Unfinished width of quilt top: _____
Add: Width of cut border strips x 2: _____
Add: _____ 4"

....

Length to cut top- and bottom-border strips: _____

3. Measure to find the center of each edge of the quilt top and lightly mark with a pencil.

4. Fold a border strip in half and pencil-mark the edge at the center. Measure out on each side of the center mark half the length of the quilt top and pencil-mark the edge of the border to mark the length of the quilt top. Pin the border strip to the side edge, matching the top and bottom edges of the quilt top with the pencil marks near the ends of the border strip and matching the center pencil mark on the quilt top with the center mark on the border strip.

5. Begin sewing ¼" from the edge of the quilt top. Stop sewing ¼" from the opposite end of the quilt top, backstitching to secure the seams at the beginning and end.

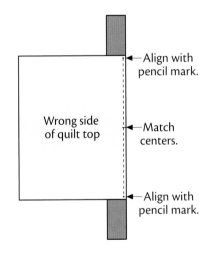

Align with pencil mark.

Wrong side of quilt top

Match centers.

Align with pencil mark.

6. Repeat steps 4 and 5 to add the remaining side border, and then add the top and bottom borders in the same manner. Press the seam allowances toward the borders.

7. After the borders have been sewn to the quilt top, fold the quilt top diagonally with the right sides together as shown. Align the seams and the edges of the borders as evenly as possible. Finger-press the seam allowances of the border away from you. Place pins in the border and on the fold as shown.

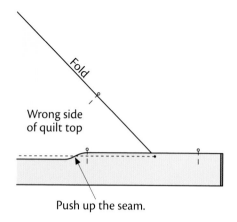

Push up the seam.

8. Align a ruler along the edge of the fold, with the 45° line along the edge of the border. Draw a line across the border along the ruler with a pencil. Place pins on the drawn line to keep the fabric from shifting.

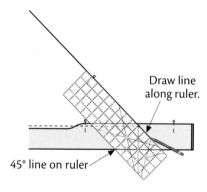

9. Begin sewing on the drawn line, backstitching at the beginning to secure the stitching. Continue to sew until you reach the edge of the border, and then backstitch to secure the seam.

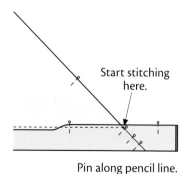

Pin along pencil line.

10. Unfold the quilt to check the accuracy of your miter. Trim away the excess fabric, leaving a ¼" seam allowance. Press the seam allowance in either direction and press the border seam allowances back in place. Repeat from step 7 to miter the remaining corners.

PREPARING THE BACKING AND BATTING

Your quilt backing needs to be 4" larger than the quilt top on all sides. Because all of the quilts in this book are wider than 42", you will need to either piece the backing or purchase a special extra-wide fabric designed for backing quilts to achieve the required width and length. To piece the backing, sew lengths of your backing fabric together. The seam can be horizontal or vertical on the quilt back. Remove the selvage edges with scissors or a rotary cutter before sewing the lengths together. Press the seam allowance in either direction.

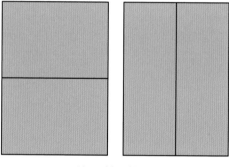

Pieced backings

If you are working with a packaged batting, take it out of the package the day before you layer your quilt and let the batting lie flat for 24 hours to relax the wrinkles. You can also fluff it in the dryer on the lowest setting for about 15 minutes. Cut your batting so it is 2" larger than your quilt top on each side. Cutting the batting slightly smaller than the backing allows you to see the backing and to make sure the edges don't accidentally fold onto themselves and get caught in the quilting.

LAYERING AND BASTING

1. Place the prepared backing wrong side up on a large, flat surface. I like to do this on the floor, but you could also use a large table, or even two utility tables pushed together. Smooth out the fabric until it lies flat. Use painter's tape on the outside edges of the backing to secure it to the floor or table. Make sure the backing is flat and taut, but not stretched.

2. Center the batting on top of the backing, smoothing out any wrinkles.

3. Center the pressed quilt top over the batting, right side up.

4. To baste for hand quilting, use a long needle and light-colored thread. Taking large stitches, work in a grid formation by stitching vertical lines approximately 4" apart, and then stitching in horizontal lines.

  To baste for machine quilting, pin the layers together using quilter's safety pins spaced approximately 4" apart.

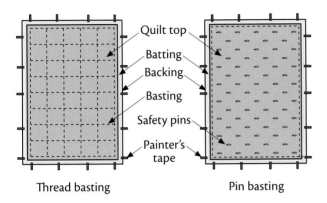

Thread basting   Pin basting

QUILTING

After your quilt has been layered and basted, you're ready to begin quilting. Generally I prefer to machine quilt my scrap quilts using an allover free-motion design with a neutral thread that blends well with the fabrics in the quilt. I like to see the "puff" in the design while minimizing the visibility of the lines of the thread. Scrap quilts can appear busy and chaotic, and I like the quilting to be subtle.

  Sometimes I quilt in the ditch along the inner and outer borders. Most of the time, however, I'll quilt an allover design right over the borders as if they were the same as the inside of the quilt. If you use a thread in a neutral color, the quilting design crossing the inner border probably won't be noticeable, and you'll spend less time quilting once you get into the rhythm of working on the same design over and over.

  If you're timid about free-motion quilting, try using a walking foot to quilt in the ditch of the seam line. For a more whimsical look, try stitching random wavy lines vertically and horizontally across the quilt.

BINDING

All of the quilts in this book were made using double-fold, straight-grain binding. The most common measurement for cutting this type of binding is 2½", and the yardage requirements and cutting instructions provide for that measurement. However, I prefer to use a narrower binding. If you like a narrower binding as well, cut your strips 2" or 2¼". You'll use a little less fabric than specified in the yardage requirements.

1. To join the binding strips, place one strip on top of the other, right sides together as shown. Sew a diagonal seam from one intersection to the other. Trim the seam allowances to ¼"; press the seam allowances open to reduce bulk.

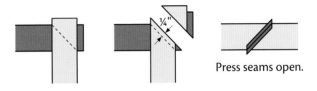

Press seams open.

2. Press the binding strip in half lengthwise with wrong sides together, aligning the long edges of the strip.

3. Using a rotary cutter, carefully trim the batting and backing away from the quilt so that all layers are even with the quilt top and the corners are square.

4. Using a walking foot or even-feed foot and a ¼" seam allowance, begin sewing the binding to the quilt along the bottom edge, leaving about 10" of the binding free. Backstitch at the beginning of the seam to secure it. Continue stitching to the corner of the quilt, stopping exactly ¼" from the edge. Backstitch to secure the seam, and then remove the quilt from the machine and clip the threads.

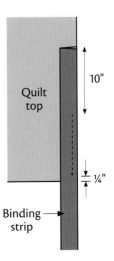

5. Rotate the quilt counterclockwise a quarter turn. Fold the binding up and away from you, finger-pressing a crease in the 45° fold. Holding the fold in place, fold the binding down and toward you, aligning the second fold with the upper edge of the quilt. Begin stitching again at the top edge of the quilt, backstitching to secure the seam.

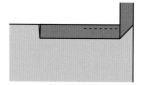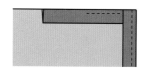

6. Continue to sew around the quilt, mitering all of the corners, until you have sewn to within approximately 12" from where you began. Backstitch to secure the seam.

7. Position the unattached binding flat on the quilt top as if it were sewn down, overlapping one end on top of the other. Trim the top end so that it overlaps the bottom end by 2½" (or the measurement of the width of your binding strip).

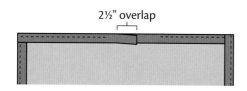

2½" overlap

8. Open both ends of the binding and position them right sides together at right angles. Draw a diagonal line as shown and pin together.

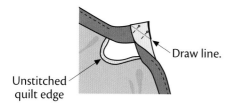

Draw line.

Unstitched quilt edge

9. Stitch on the drawn line. Before trimming, open the binding and check to ensure that you've sewn the binding ends together correctly. (Don't ask me why I suggest that you do this.) Trim the seam allowances to ¼" and press them open.

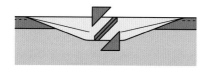

Trim to ¼" and press open.

10. Fold the binding back in place and finish stitching it to the quilt.

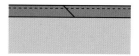

11. Fold the binding to the back of the quilt. Sew the binding down by hand using an appliqué or blind hem stitch. Miter the corners as shown.

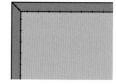

Quilt back

LABELING YOUR QUILT

Adding a label to the back of your quilt is a good way to document its history for future generations. To make a label, cut a piece of muslin or light-colored fabric the desired size plus ¼" on all sides. Place the label face down on an ironing board and iron a piece of freezer paper (waxy side down!) to the back of the label. This will provide a more stable surface for writing. Use a fine-point permanent pigment marker to write on your label, leaving margins approximately ½" on all sides of the label. It doesn't have to be a work of art, but it should provide some basic information about the quilt, such as:

- The name of the person for whom the quilt was made and the recipient's city and state

- The maker's name plus city and state

- An event that inspired the quilt, such as a birthday or other celebration

- The date the quilt was finished

- Drawings or doodles

Once you have finished writing on your label, remove the freezer paper. Press the edges of the label ¼" toward the back all the way around to hide the raw edges. Attach the label to the back of the quilt (preferably in a lower corner) by using an appliqué stitch or a whipstitch. You're now ready to enjoy your finished quilt!

Special Piecing Techniques

Triangle-free piecing techniques have been used throughout this book to create triangles and trapezoid shapes by using only squares and rectangles.

FOLDED-CORNER UNITS

There are several methods that you could use to achieve the same result, but my two favorite methods for making folded-corner units are explained below.

Marking

Using a small ruler and a mechanical pencil, draw a diagonal line from corner to corner on the wrong side of a 2½" fabric square. Place the square on top of a fabric rectangle, right sides together and corners aligned, for folded-corner units (or on top of another square for half-square-triangle units) and sew on the drawn line. Fold up the square and match the corners and edges to make sure you've sewn accurately. If your corners don't meet, you may need to adjust your seam by sewing the width of a thread or two toward the upper corner. If your corners meet, press the triangle in place. Fold the triangle back down and trim the excess fabric, leaving ¼" seam allowances. Press back into place.

  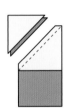

| Sew on the diagonal line. | Check accuracy. | Trim seam allowances. | Press back into place. |

No Marking

If you don't enjoy marking the diagonal lines on your folded corners, try making a temporary seam guide. Cut a piece of painter's tape about 3½" to 4" long. Place the tape on the bed of your sewing machine, lining up one long edge with the needle and making sure that the tape doesn't touch the feed dogs. Place the point of the unit to be sewn directly in front of the needle and make sure the other point is lined up with the edge of the painter's tape. Sew the unit, guiding the opposite point along the edge of the tape until it reaches the needle.

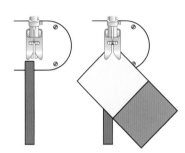

SPLIT UNITS

Split units are similar to folded-corner units. Instead of sewing a square to a rectangle or another square, two rectangles are sewn together at right angles to produce a unit that appears to be split diagonally in the middle. To make these units, place two fabric rectangles right sides together, at right angles, matching the corners. Draw a diagonal line from corner to corner. Sew on the drawn line. Fold the strip up and check to make sure you've sewn accurately. Trim the excess corner fabric, leaving ¼" seam allowances. Press the seam allowances toward the darker fabric or press as indicated in the project instructions.

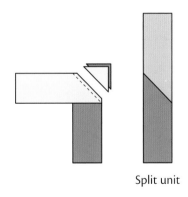

Split unit

Town Square

Pieced and quilted by Kim Brackett

The folded-corner rectangle units on the outer edges of the blocks in this quilt appear to form a triangle, creating the illusion that the squares are floating on top.

FINISHED QUILT: 63½" x 63½" ❖ FINISHED BLOCK: 6" x 6"

MATERIALS

Yardages are based on 42"-wide fabric.
24 strips, 2½" x 42", of assorted dark prints in reds, blues, browns, and greens for blocks
1⅔ yards of cream print for blocks
1⅔ yards of large-scale floral for outer border and binding
⅓ yard of red print for inner border
4¼ yards of fabric for backing
67½" x 67½" piece of batting

CUTTING

From *each* of 12 assorted dark print strips, cut:
2 rectangles, 2½" x 6½" (24 total)
3 rectangles, 2½" x 4½" (36 total)
4 squares, 2½" x 2½" (48 total)

From *each* of the remaining 12 assorted dark print strips, cut:
1 rectangle, 2½" x 6½" (12 total)
3 rectangles, 2½" x 4½" (36 total)
6 squares, 2½" x 2½" (72 total)

From the remainder of 1 dark print strip, cut:
1 square, 2½" x 2½" (If you don't have a leftover strip that is long enough to cut this square, use a scrap from either of your border prints.)

From the cream print, cut:
21 strips, 2½" x 42"; crosscut into:
    84 rectangles, 2½" x 6½"
    108 squares, 2½" x 2½"

From the red print, cut:
6 border strips, 1½" x 42"

From the large-scale floral, cut:
6 border strips, 6" x 42"
7 binding strips, 2½" x 42"

CUTTING FROM SCRAPS

If you prefer to use scraps, follow the instructions below, cutting the pieces in each set from the same fabric. See "Cutting" at left for instructions on cutting the borders and binding.

From assorted dark prints, cut:
36 squares, 2½" x 2½"
36 sets of:
    1 rectangle, 2½" x 4½"
    1 square, 2½" x 2½"
36 sets of:
    1 rectangle, 2½" x 6½"
    1 rectangle, 2½" x 4½"
49 squares, 2½" x 2½"

From assorted cream prints, cut:
108 squares, 2½" x 2½"
84 rectangles, 2½" x 6½"

BLOCK ASSEMBLY

1. Referring to "Folded-Corner Units" on page 17 and using one dark and one cream 2½" square, make a half-square-triangle unit. Press the seam allowance toward the dark triangle. Make 36.

Make 36.

2. Select a dark 2½" square and a matching 2½" x 4½" rectangle. Sew the square to the cream side of a half-square-triangle unit from step 1. Press the seam allowance toward the square. Add the matching rectangle to the top of the unit. Press the seam allowance toward the rectangle. Repeat with the remaining units from step 1.

Make 36.

3. Select a dark 2½" x 4½" rectangle and a matching 2½" x 6½" rectangle. Make folded-corner units as shown using the rectangles and cream 2½" squares. Press the seam allowances toward the cream triangles. Make 36 matching pairs.

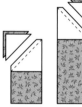 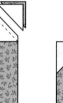 

Make 36
matching pairs.

4. Working with matching pairs of units from step 3, sew the 2½" x 4½" folded-corner unit to the side of a unit from step 2. Press the seam allowance toward the folded-corner unit. Sew the remaining folded-corner unit to the top of the unit. Press the seam allowance toward the folded-corner unit. Make 36 blocks.

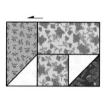 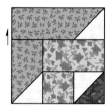

Make 36.

QUILT ASSEMBLY AND FINISHING

1. Arrange the blocks, the cream 2½" x 6½" sashing strips, and the dark 2½" sashing posts as shown. Sew the units together in horizontal rows, pressing the seam allowances as shown. Sew the rows together. Press the seam allowances in the same direction.

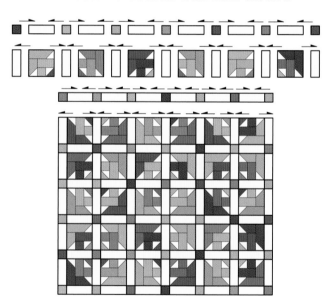

2. Referring to "Butted-Corner Borders" on page 12, add the red 1½"-wide inner-border strips and the floral 6"-wide outer-border strips.
3. Layer the quilt top, batting, and backing; baste the layers together. Quilt as desired.
4. Referring to "Binding" on page 15 and using the floral 2½"-wide strips, bind the edges of the quilt.
5. Add a label.

Pieced and quilted by Karen Williamson

When Karen became a grandmother she asked to be called "Nana," but it wasn't long after her granddaughter learned to talk that the child began calling Karen "Nana Girl."

FINISHED QUILT: 56½" x 66½" ❖ FINISHED BLOCK: 8" x 8"

MATERIALS

Yardages are based on 42"-wide fabric.

20 strips, 2½" x 42", of assorted dark prints in pinks, reds, browns, and golds for blocks

2 yards of pale yellow marbled print for blocks, sashing strips, and sashing posts

1 ⅓ yards of large-scale floral for outer border

½ yard of green print for sashing strip "leaves"

⅜ yard of brown print for inner border

⅝ yard of pink print for binding

4 yards of fabric for backing

60½" x 71½" piece of batting

CUTTING

From *each* of the 20 assorted dark print strips, cut:
8 rectangles, 2½" x 4½" (160 total)

From the pale yellow marbled print, cut:
13 strips, 2½" x 42"; crosscut into 49 rectangles, 2½" x 8½"
12 strips, 2½" x 42"; crosscut into 190 squares, 2½" x 2½"

From the green print, cut:
6 strips, 2½" x 42"; crosscut into 80 squares, 2½" x 2½"

From the brown print, cut:
5 border strips, 2" x 42"

From the large-scale floral, cut:
7 border strips, 6" x 42"

From the pink print, cut:
7 binding strips, 2½" x 42"

BLOCK ASSEMBLY

1. Referring to "Folded-Corner Units" on page 17 and using one dark 2½" x 4½" rectangle and two pale yellow 2½" squares, make a folded-corner unit as shown. Press the seam allowances toward the pale yellow triangles. Make four identical units for each of the 20 blocks.

Make 4
for each block.

2. Sew a matching 2½" x 4½" rectangle to the top of each unit from step 1. Press the seam allowances toward the rectangles.

Make 4
for each block.

3. Sew together four matching units from step 2 as shown. Press the seam allowances as shown. Make 20 blocks.

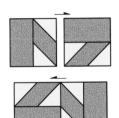

Make 20.

SASHING STRIP ASSEMBLY

1. Referring to "Folded-Corner Units" on page 17 and using a pale yellow 2½" x 8½" rectangle and a green print 2½" square, make a folded-corner unit as shown. Press the seam allowance toward the green triangle. Make 18.

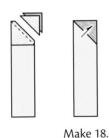

Make 18.

2. Make a folded-corner unit as shown using a pale yellow 2½" x 8½" rectangle and two green print 2½" squares. Press the seam allowances toward the green triangles. Make 31.

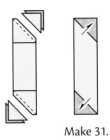

Make 31.

QUILT ASSEMBLY AND FINISHING

1. Arrange the blocks, pieced sashing strips, and cream 2½" sashing posts as shown. Sew the units together in horizontal rows, pressing the seam allowances as shown. Sew the rows together. Press the seam allowances in the same direction.

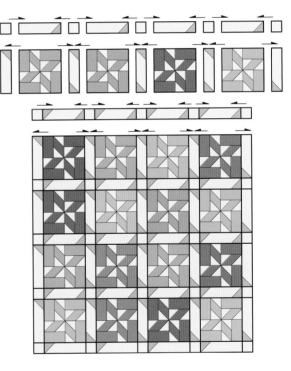

2. Referring to "Butted-Corner Borders" on page 12, add the brown 2"-wide inner-border strips.
3. Referring to "Mitered-Corner Borders" on page 13, add the floral 6"-wide outer-border strips.
4. Layer the quilt top, batting, and backing; baste the layers together. Quilt as desired.
5. Referring to "Binding" on page 15 and using the pink print 2½"-wide strips, bind the edges of the quilt.
6. Add a label.

Pieced and quilted by Darlene Johannis

Darlene stepped outside of her comfort zone to make this quilt entirely from random scraps instead of a single fabric collection. I love looking at all the different fabrics she used in the blocks.

FINISHED QUILT: 54½" x 62½" ❖ FINISHED BLOCK: 8" x 8"

MATERIALS

Yardages are based on 42"-wide fabric.
30 strips, at least 2½" x 31", of assorted dark prints for blocks
30 strips, at least 2½" x 31", of assorted light prints for blocks
1¾ yards of red print for outer border and binding
⅓ yard of black print for inner border
4 yards of fabric for backing
58½" x 66½" piece of batting

CUTTING

From each of the 30 assorted dark print strips, cut:
8 rectangles, 2½" x 3½" (240 total)

From each of the 30 assorted light print strips, cut:
8 rectangles, 2½" x 3½" (240 total)

From the black print, cut:
5 border strips, 1½" x 42"

From the red print, cut:
6 border strips, 6½" x 42"
7 binding strips, 2½" x 42"

CUTTING FROM SCRAPS

If you prefer to use scraps, follow the instructions below. See "Cutting" at left for instructions on cutting the borders and binding.

From assorted dark prints, cut:
60 *sets* of 4 matching rectangles, 2½" x 3½" (240 total)

From assorted light prints, cut:
30 *sets* of 8 matching rectangles, 2½" x 3½" (240 total)

BLOCK ASSEMBLY

1. Select eight matching light 2½" x 3½" rectangles and two sets of four matching dark 2½" x 3½" rectangles. Referring to "Split Units" on page 17, make split units using one dark and one light rectangle for each unit. Press the seam allowances toward the dark fabrics. Make two sets of four matching units for each of the 30 blocks.

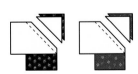

Make 2 sets of 4 for each block.

2. Sew together one of each split unit from each block set as shown. Make four units for each block. Press the seam allowances in the same direction for each set of split units.

Make 4
for each block.

3. Sew together the four units from step 2 as shown. Refer to "Pressing" on page 11 to press the seam allowances in a clockwise direction. Make 30 blocks.

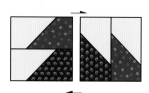

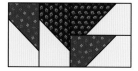

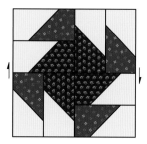

Make 30.

QUILT ASSEMBLY AND FINISHING

1. Arrange the blocks in six horizontal rows of five blocks each. Sew the blocks together in rows, pressing the seam allowances in alternating directions from row to row. Sew the rows together. Press the seam allowances in the same direction.

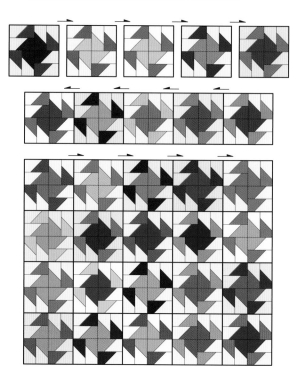

2. Referring to "Butted-Corner Borders" on page 12, add the black 1½"-wide inner-border strips and the red 6½"-wide outer-border strips.
3. Layer the quilt top, batting, and backing; baste the layers together. Quilt as desired.
4. Referring to "Binding" on page 15 and using the red 2½"-wide strips, bind the edges of the quilt.
5. Add a label.

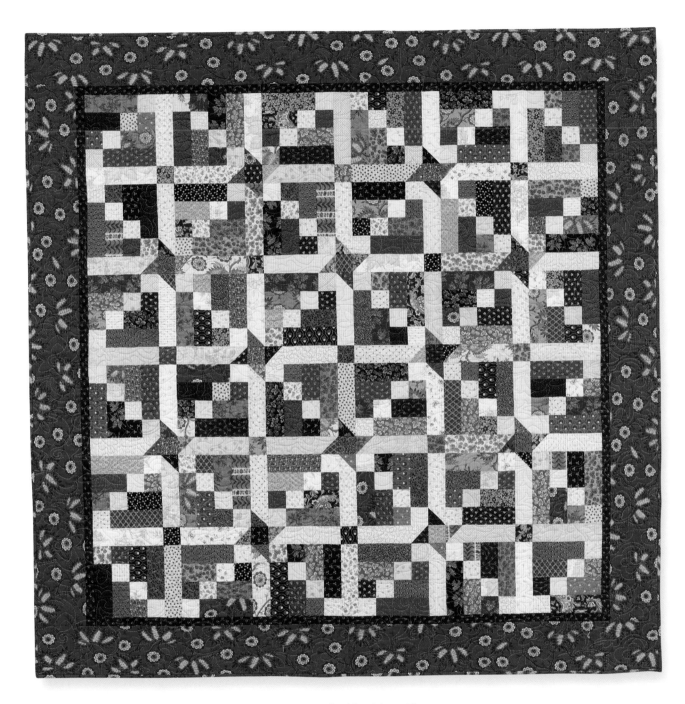

Pieced and quilted by Mary Flynn

Mary used lots of Civil War–era reproduction prints in her quilt for a warm, rich look. If you prefer a contemporary look, try using bright fabrics with a single light background print. Just cut the number of rectangles and squares provided for the assorted cream prints in "Cutting from Scraps."

FINISHED QUILT: 71½" x 71½" ❖ FINISHED BLOCK: 8" x 8"

MATERIALS

Yardages are based on 42"-wide fabric.
31 strips, 2½" x 42", of assorted dark prints for blocks
24 strips, 2½" x 42", of assorted cream prints for blocks
2 yards of red floral for outer border and binding
⅓ yard of dark brown print for inner border
5 yards of fabric for backing
75½" x 75½" piece of batting

CUTTING

From *each* of 10 assorted dark print strips, cut:
3 rectangles, 2½" x 6½" (30 total)
2 rectangles, 2½" x 4½" (20 total)
4 squares, 2½" x 2½" (40 total)

From *each* of 10 different assorted dark print strips, cut:
2 rectangles, 2½" x 6½" (20 total)
3 rectangles, 2½" x 4½" (30 total)
4 squares, 2½" x 2½" (40 total)

From *each* of the remaining 11 assorted dark print strips, cut:
2 rectangles, 2½" x 6½" (22 total)
2 rectangles, 2½" x 4½" (22 total)
6 squares, 2½" x 2½" (66 total; you will have 1 left over)

From *each* of 14 assorted cream print strips, cut:
3 rectangles, 2½" x 8½" (42 total)
5 squares, 2½" x 2½" (70 total)

From *each* of the remaining 10 assorted cream print strips, cut:
2 rectangles, 2½" x 8½" (20 total; you will have 2 left over)
8 squares, 2½" x 2½" (80 total; you will have 6 left over)

From the dark brown print, cut:
6 border strips, 1½" x 42"

From the red floral, cut:
7 border strips, 6" x 42"
8 binding strips, 2½" x 42"

CUTTING FROM SCRAPS

If you prefer to use scraps, follow the instructions below. See "Cutting" at left for instructions on cutting the borders and binding.

From assorted dark prints, cut:
72 rectangles, 2½" x 6½"
72 rectangles, 2½" x 4½"
145 squares, 2½" x 2½"

From assorted cream prints, cut:
60 rectangles, 2½" x 8½"
144 squares, 2½" x 2½"

BLOCK ASSEMBLY

1. Sew a cream 2½" square to a dark print 2½" x 6½" rectangle as shown. Press the seam allowance toward the rectangle. Make 72.

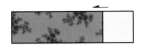

Make 72.

2. Sew together a dark print 2½" square, a cream 2½" square, and a dark print 2½" x 4½" rectangle as shown. Press the seam allowances toward the dark prints. Make 72.

Make 72.

3. Sew together two units from step 1 and two units from step 2 as shown. Press the seam allowances as shown. Make 36 blocks.

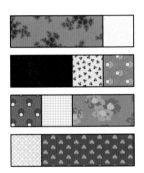 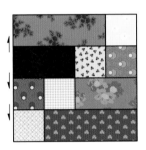

Make 36.

SASHING STRIP ASSEMBLY

Referring to "Folded-Corner Units" on page 17 and using one cream print 2½" x 8½" rectangle and one dark 2½" square, make a folded-corner unit as shown. Press the seam allowance toward the dark triangle. Make 48.

Make 48.

QUILT ASSEMBLY AND FINISHING

1. Arrange the blocks, pieced sashing strips, the remaining cream 2½" x 8½" rectangles, and the remaining dark print 2½" squares as shown. Sew the units together in horizontal rows, pressing the seam allowances as shown. Sew the rows together. Press the seam allowances in the same direction.

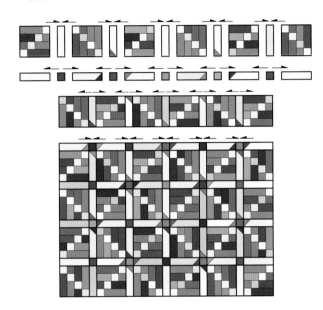

2. Referring to "Butted-Corner Borders" on page 12, add the dark brown 1½"-wide inner-border strips and the red floral 6"-wide outer-border strips.
3. Layer the quilt top, batting, and backing; baste the layers together. Quilt as desired.
4. Referring to "Binding" on page 15 and using the red floral 2½"-wide strips, bind the edges of the quilt.
5. Add a label.

Pieced and quilted by Kim Brackett

Using a solid white background allows even large-scale prints to stand out, and it provides a nice contrast for the main fabrics.

FINISHED QUILT: 61½" x 61½" ❖ FINISHED BLOCK: 12" x 12"

MATERIALS

Yardages are based on 42"-wide fabric.

26 strips, 2½" x 42", of assorted dark prints in blues and greens for blocks

1⅛ yards of white solid for blocks

1⅛ yards of floral for outer border

⅓ yard of blue-and-green striped fabric for inner border

⅝ yard of blue-and-green print for binding

4¼ yards of fabric for backing

65½" x 65½" piece of batting

CUTTING

From *each of 20 assorted dark print strips*, cut:

4 rectangles, 2½" x 6½" (80 total; you will have 2 left over)

1 rectangle, 2½" x 4½" (20 total)

2 squares, 2½" x 2½" (40 total)

From *each of the remaining 6 assorted dark print strips*, cut:

3 rectangles, 2½" x 6½" (18 total)

2 rectangles, 2½" x 4½" (12 total)

4 squares, 2½" x 2½" (24 total)

From the white solid, cut:

4 strips, 4½" x 42"; crosscut into 32 squares, 4½" x 4½"

7 strips, 2½" x 42"; crosscut into 96 squares, 2½" x 2½"

From the blue-and-green striped fabric, cut:

5 border strips, 1½" x 42"

From the floral, cut:

6 border strips, 6" x 42"

From the blue-and-green print, cut:

7 binding strips, 2½" x 42"

QUILT ASSEMBLY AND FINISHING

1. Referring to "Folded-Corner Units" on page 17 and using one blue or green print 2½" x 4½" rectangle and one white solid 2½" square, make a folded-corner unit as shown. Press the seam allowance toward the white triangle. Make 32.

Make 32.

2. Sew the folded-corner unit from step 1 to a white solid 4½" square. Press the seam allowance toward the square. Make 32.

Make 32.

3. Make a folded-corner unit as shown using a blue or green print 2½" x 6½" rectangle and a white solid 2½" square. Press the seam allowance toward the white triangle. Make 32.

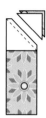

Make 32.

4. Sew the unit from step 3 to the unit from step 2. Press the seam allowance toward the unit from step 3. Make 32.

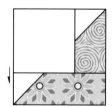

Make 32.

5. Sew blue or green print 2½" squares to the top and bottom of a white solid 2½" square. Press the seam allowances toward the blue or green squares. Make 32.

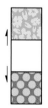

Make 32.

6. Sew blue or green print 2½" x 6½" rectangles to each side of the unit from step 5. Press the seam allowances toward the rectangles. Make 32.

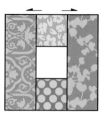

Make 32.

7. Sew together two units from step 4 and two units from step 6 as shown. Refer to "Pressing" on page 11 to press the seam allowances in a clockwise direction. Make 16 blocks.

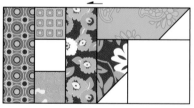

Make 16.

QUILT ASSEMBLY AND FINISHING

1. Arrange the blocks into four horizontal rows of four blocks each as shown. Sew the blocks together in rows, pressing the seam allowances as shown. Sew the rows together. Press the seam allowances in the same direction.

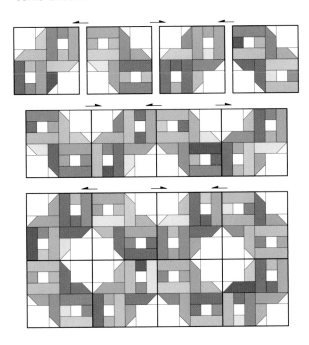

2. Referring to "Butted-Corner Borders" on page 12, add the blue-and-green striped 1½"-wide inner-border strips and the floral 6"-wide outer-border strips.
3. Layer the quilt top, batting, and backing; baste the layers together. Quilt as desired.
4. Referring to "Binding" on page 15 and using the blue-and-green print 2½"-wide strips, bind the edges of the quilt.
5. Add a label.

Nova

Pieced by Kim Brackett; quilted by Karen Williamson

The blocks in this quilt appear to be offset, lending movement to the stars. To re-create this quilt, use a variety of batiks in subtle, muted shades.

FINISHED QUILT: 61½" x 77½" ❖ FINISHED BLOCK: 8" x 8"

MATERIALS

Yardages are based on 42"-wide fabric.
32 strips, 2½" x 42", of assorted dark batiks for blocks
2⅓ yards of light batik for blocks
1⅓ yards of multicolored batik for outer border
1 yard of rust batik for inner border and binding
4¼ yards of fabric for backing
65½" x 81 ½" piece of batting

CUTTING

From each of 16 assorted dark batik strips, cut:
2 rectangles, 2½" x 8½" (32 total)
1 rectangle, 2½" x 6½" (16 total)
1 rectangle, 2½" x 4½" (16 total)
4 squares, 2½" x 2½" (64 total)

From each of the remaining 16 dark batik strips, cut:
1 rectangle, 2½" x 8½" (16 total)
2 rectangles, 2½" x 6½" (32 total)
2 rectangles, 2½" x 4½" (32 total)
2 squares, 2½" x 2½" (32 total)

From the light batik, cut:
30 strips, 2½" x 42"; crosscut into:
    48 rectangles, 2½" x 6½"
    336 squares, 2½" x 2½"

From the rust batik, cut:
6 border strips, 1½" x 42"
8 binding strips, 2½" x 42"

From the multicolored batik, cut:
7 border strips, 6" x 42"

BLOCK ASSEMBLY

1. Referring to "Folded-Corner Units" on page 17 and using one dark batik and one light batik 2½" square, make a half-square-triangle unit. Press the seam allowance toward the dark triangle. Make 96.

Make 96.

2. Sew a light batik 2½" square to the dark side of a half-square-triangle unit from step 1. Press the seam allowances toward the square. Make 96.

Make 96.

3. Sew together two units from step 2. Refer to "Pressing" on page 11 to press the seam allowances in a clockwise direction. Make 48.

Make 48.

4. Using a dark batik 2½" x 4½" rectangle and a light batik 2½" square, make a folded-corner unit as shown. Press the seam allowance toward the light triangle. Make 48.

Make 48.

5. Sew a unit from step 4 to a unit from step 3 as shown. Press the seam allowance toward the unit from step 4. Make 48.

Make 48.

6. Make a folded-corner unit as shown using a dark batik 2½" x 6½" rectangle and a light batik 2½" square. Press the seam allowance toward the light triangle. Make 48.

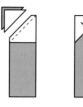

Make 48.

7. Sew a unit from step 6 to a unit from step 5 as shown. Press the seam allowance toward the unit from step 6. Make 48.

Make 48.

8. Sew a light batik 2½" x 6½" rectangle to the top of the unit from step 7. Press the seam allowance toward the rectangle. Make 48.

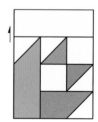

Make 48.

9. Make a folded-corner unit as shown using a dark batik 2½" x 8½" rectangle and a light batik 2½" square. Press the seam allowance toward the light triangle. Make 48.

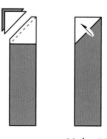

Make 48.

10. Sew a unit from step 9 to a unit from step 8 as shown. Press the seam allowance toward the unit from step 9. Make 48 blocks.

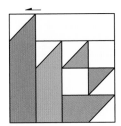

Make 48.

QUILT ASSEMBLY AND FINISHING

1. Arrange the blocks in eight horizontal rows of six blocks each as shown. Sew the blocks together in rows, pressing the seam allowances as shown. Sew the rows together. Press the seam allowances in the same direction.

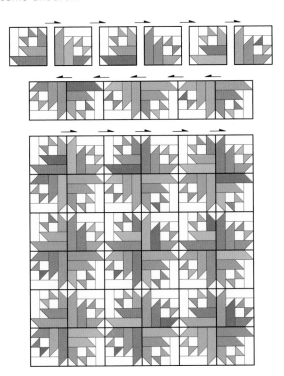

2. Referring to "Butted-Corner Borders" on page 12, add the rust batik 1½"-wide inner-border strips and the multicolored batik 6"-wide outer-border strips.
3. Layer the quilt top, batting, and backing; baste the layers together. Quilt as desired.
4. Referring to "Binding" on page 15 and using the rust batik 2½"-wide strips, bind the edges of the quilt.
5. Add a label.

Pieced and quilted by Mary Flynn

Mary used two rolls of precut strips from the same fabric collection to make this quilt. The pieced border is my favorite part of this quilt, but if you don't have the time or patience to piece the border, substitute a plain border instead.

FINISHED QUILT: 52½" x 66½" ❖ FINISHED BLOCK: 14" x 14"

MATERIALS

Yardages are based on 42"-wide fabric.
12 *pairs* of strips, 2½" x 42", of assorted dark prints in blues, reds, browns, greens, and blacks for block stars and pieced outer border
12 *pairs* of strips, 2½" x 42", of assorted dark prints in blues, reds, browns, greens, and blacks for block centers, block frames, and pieced outer border
12 *pairs* of strips, 2½" x 42", of assorted light tan prints for block backgrounds and pieced outer border
⅓ yard of light tan print for inner border
⅝ yard of green print for binding
3½ yards of fabric for backing
56½" x 70½" piece of batting

CUTTING

For ease in piecing, keep together the pieces that you cut from each pair of assorted dark strips and each pair of assorted light tan strips. Label the dark sets with their intended placement in the block (stars or centers and frames) to avoid mixing up the sets.

From *each* of the 12 pairs of assorted dark strips for block stars, cut:
4 rectangles, 2½" x 6½" (48 total)
4 rectangles, 2½" x 4½" (48 total)

From *each* of the 12 pairs of assorted dark strips for block centers and block frames, cut:
4 rectangles, 2½" x 6½" (48 total)
4 rectangles, 2½" x 4½" (48 total)
1 square, 2½" x 2½" (12 total)

From the remainder of the dark strips, cut a *total* of:
106 rectangles, 2½" x 4½"
6 squares, 2½" x 2½"

From *each* of the 12 pairs of assorted light tan strips, cut:
4 rectangles, 2½" x 4½" (48 total)
12 squares, 2½" x 2½" (144 total)

From the remainder of the assorted light tan strips, cut a *total* of:
114 squares, 2½" x 2½"

From the light tan print, cut:
6 border strips, 1½" x 42"

From the green print, cut:
7 binding strips, 2½" x 42"

CUTTING FROM SCRAPS

If you prefer to use scraps, follow the instructions below. See "Cutting" on page 39 for instructions on cutting the inner border and binding.

For blocks

From *each* of 12 assorted dark prints for block stars, cut:
4 rectangles, 2½" x 6½" (48 total)
4 rectangles, 2½" x 4½" (48 total)

From *each* of 12 assorted dark prints for block centers and frames, cut:
4 rectangles, 2½" x 6½" (48 total)
4 rectangles, 2½" x 4½" (48 total)
1 square, 2½" x 2½" (12 total)

From *each* of 12 assorted light prints, cut:
4 rectangles, 2½" x 4½" (48 total)
12 squares, 2½" x 2½" (144 total)

For pieced border

From assorted dark prints, cut:
106 rectangles, 2½" x 4½"
6 squares, 2½" x 2½"

From assorted light prints, cut:
114 squares, 2½" x 2½"

BLOCK ASSEMBLY

1. Select one set of block star pieces, one set of light tan background pieces, and one set of block center and frame pieces.
2. Referring to "Folded-Corner Units" on page 17, make a folded-corner unit as shown using a dark print 2½" x 4½" rectangle from the block star set and an assorted light tan print 2½" square. Press the seam allowance toward the light triangle. Make four identical units.

Make 4.

3. Sew a matching light print 2½" x 4½" rectangle to each unit from step 2. Press the seam allowances toward the rectangles.

Make 4.

4. Sew a dark print 2½" x 4½" rectangle from the block frame set to each unit from step 3 as shown. Press the seam allowances toward the rectangles.

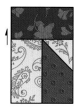

Make 4.

5. Sew a matching dark print 2½" x 6½" rectangle to each unit from step 4 as shown. Press the seam allowances toward the rectangles.

Make 4.

6. Make a double folded-corner unit as shown using a dark print 2½" x 6½" rectangle from the block star set and two light tan 2½" squares. Press the seam allowances toward the light triangles. Make four identical units.

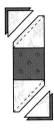

Make 4.

7. Sew a unit from step 5 to each side of a unit from step 6. Make two. Press the seam allowances *open*.

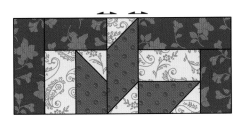

Make 2.

8. Sew the remaining two units from step 6 to the sides of the dark 2½" square from the block frame set. Press the seam allowances *open*.

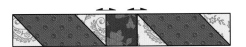

Make 1.

9. Sew together the units from steps 7 and 8 as shown. Press the seam allowances *open*.

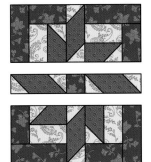

10. Repeat steps 1–9 to make a total of 12 blocks.

QUILT ASSEMBLY AND FINISHING

1. Arrange the blocks in four horizontal rows of three blocks each. Sew the blocks together in rows, pressing the seam allowances in alternating directions from row to row. Sew the rows together. Press the seam allowances in the same direction.

2. Sew the six light tan 1½" x 42" strips together end to end. From the pieced strip, cut two strips 56½" long and two strips 44½" long.

3. Join the 56½"-long strips to the sides of the quilt top. Press the seam allowances toward the strips. Join the 44½"-long strips to the top and bottom of the quilt top. Press the seam allowances toward the strips.

4. Make folded-corner units as shown using the assorted dark print 2½" x 4½" rectangles and the assorted light tan print 2½" squares. Be sure the stitching line is positioned correctly for the A and B units. Make 54 A units and 50 B units. Press the seam allowances toward the light triangles.

Unit A.
Make 54.

Unit B.
Make 50.

5. Referring to "Folded-Corner Units," make a half-square-triangle unit using a dark print 2½" square and a light print 2½" square. Press the seam allowance toward the dark triangle. Make six.

Make 6.

6. Sew a light tan 2½" square to a half-square-triangle unit from step 5. Press the seam allowance toward the square. Make four units.

Make 4.

7. Sew a folded-corner A unit from step 4 to a unit from step 6 to make a corner unit. Make four.

Make 4.

8. Place a half-square-triangle unit from step 5 on one end of a dark print 2½" x 4½" rectangle as shown, right sides together. Sew diagonally from corner to corner. Trim the seam allowance to ¼". Press the seam allowance toward the rectangle. Make two.

Make 2.

9. Sew together 14 A units from step 4 along the long edges. Press the seam allowances toward the left. Sew together 14 B units from step 4 along the long edges. Press the seam allowance toward the right. Sew these strips to a unit from step 8 as shown. Press the seam allowances toward the step 8 unit. Make two side border strips.

Side border.
Make 2.

10. Sew together 11 A units from step 4 along the long edges. Press the seam allowances toward the left. Sew together 11 B units from step 4 along the long edges. Press the seam allowances toward the right. Sew these strips together, and then add a corner unit from step 7 to the ends as shown. Press the seam allowances toward the corner units. Make two top/bottom border strips.

Top/bottom border.
Make 2.

11. Sew the side border strips to the sides of the quilt top. Press the seam allowances toward the inner border. Sew the top/bottom border strips to the top and bottom of the quilt top. Press the seam allowances toward the inner border.

12. Layer the quilt top, batting, and backing; baste the layers together. Quilt as desired.
13. Referring to "Binding" on page 15 and using the green print 2½"-wide strips, bind the edges of the quilt. *Use a scant ¼" seam allowance to avoid chopping off the points of the pieced border.*
14. Add a label.

Summer Daze

Pieced and quilted by Darlene Johannis

If you want to recapture the look of Darlene's quilt, use lots of sweet 1930s reproduction prints against a solid white background.

FINISHED QUILT: 61½" x 61½" ❖ FINISHED BLOCK: 12" x 12"

MATERIALS

Yardages are based on 42"-wide fabric.

27 strips, 2½" x 42", of assorted 1930s-era reproduction prints for blocks

1⅔ yards of yellow print for outer border and binding

1⅛ yards of white solid for blocks

⅓ yard of blue print for inner border

4¼ yards of fabric for backing

65½" x 65½" piece of batting

CUTTING

From each of 9 reproduction print strips, cut:
2 rectangles, 2½" x 6½" (18 total)
2 rectangles, 2½" x 4½" (18 total)
5 squares, 2½" x 2½" (45 total)

From each of the remaining 18 reproduction print strips, cut:
1 rectangle, 2½" x 6½" (18 total; you will have 4 left over)
3 rectangles, 2½" x 4½" (54 total; you will have 8 left over)
5 squares, 2½" x 2½" (90 total; you will have 7 left over)

From the white solid, cut:
14 strips, 2½" x 42"; crosscut into:
    64 rectangles, 2½" x 4½"
    96 squares, 2½" x 2½"

From the blue print, cut:
5 border strips, 1½" x 42"

From the yellow print, cut:
6 border strips, 6" x 42"
7 binding strips, 2½" x 42"

BLOCK ASSEMBLY

1. Sew a print 2½" square to a white solid 2½" square as shown. Press the seam allowance toward the print square. Make 32.

Make 32.

2. Sew a print 2½" x 4½" rectangle to the top of a unit from step 1. Press the seam allowance toward the rectangle. Make 32.

Make 32.

3. Sew a print 2½" x 4½" rectangle to the side of a unit from step 2. Press the seam allowance toward the newly added rectangle. Make 32.

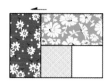

Make 32.

4. Sew a print 2½" x 6½" rectangle to the top of a unit from step 3. Press the seam allowance toward the newly added rectangle. Make 32.

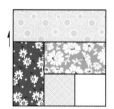

Make 32.

5. Sew a print 2½" square to a white solid 2½" x 4½" rectangle as shown. Press the seam allowance toward the square. Make 64.

Make 64.

6. Sew white solid 2½" squares to opposite sides of a print 2½" square. Press the seam allowance toward the print square. Make 32.

Make 32.

7. Sew two units from step 5 and one unit from step 6 together as shown. Press the seam allowances as shown. Make 32.

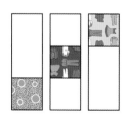

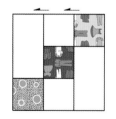

Make 32.

8. Sew together two units from step 4 and two units from step 7 as shown. Refer to "Pressing" on page 11 to press the seam allowances in a clockwise direction. Make 16 blocks.

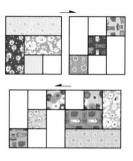

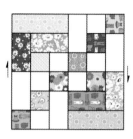

Make 16.

QUILT ASSEMBLY AND FINISHING

1. Arrange the blocks in four horizontal rows of four blocks each. Sew the blocks together in rows, pressing the seam allowances in alternate directions from row to row. Sew the rows together. Press the seam allowances in the same direction.

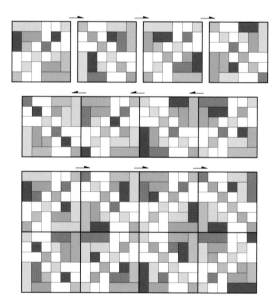

2. Referring to "Butted-Corner Borders" on page 12, add the blue 1½"-wide inner-border strips and the yellow print 6"-wide outer-border strips.

3. Layer the quilt top, batting, and backing; baste the layers together. Quilt as desired.

4. Referring to "Binding" on page 15 and using the yellow print 2½"-wide strips, bind the edges of the quilt.

5. Add a label.

Blues Crossing

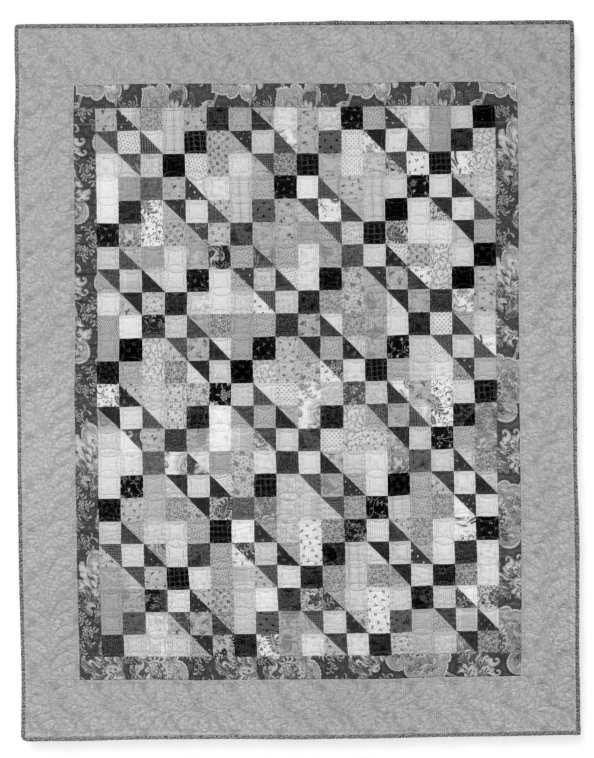

Pieced and quilted by Karen Williamson

I love the diagonal lines in this quilt created by the red triangles and blue squares. To re-create Karen's quilt, use lots of different red, blue, and tan fabrics for an old-fashioned look.

FINISHED QUILT: 51½" x 63½" ❖ FINISHED BLOCK: 6" x 6"

MATERIALS

Yardages are based on 42"-wide fabric.
24 strips, 2½" x 42", of assorted tan fabrics
7 strips, 2½" x 42", of assorted red fabrics
5 strips, 2½" x 42", of assorted blue fabrics
1⅛ yards of tan print for outer border
½ yard of red floral for inner border
⅝ yard of blue print for binding
3¾ yards of fabric for backing
55½" x 67½" piece of batting

CUTTING

From each of the 24 assorted tan strips, cut:
2 rectangles, 2½" x 4½" (48 total)
11 squares, 2½" x 2½" (264 total)

From each of the 7 assorted red strips, cut:
15 squares, 2½" x 2½" (105 total; you will have
   9 left over)

From each of the 5 assorted blue strips, cut:
15 squares, 2½" x 2½" (75 total; you will have
   3 left over)

From the red floral, cut:
6 border strips, 2½" x 42"

From the tan print, cut:
6 border strips, 6" x 42"

From the blue print, cut:
7 binding strips, 2½" x 42"

CUTTING FROM SCRAPS

If you prefer to use scraps, follow the instructions below. See "Cutting" at left for instructions on cutting the borders and binding.

From assorted tan prints, cut:
48 rectangles, 2½" x 4½"
264 squares, 2½" x 2½"

From assorted red prints, cut:
96 squares, 2½" x 2½"

From assorted blue prints, cut:
72 squares, 2½" x 2½"

BLOCK A ASSEMBLY

1. Referring to "Folded-Corner Units" on page 17, make a half-square-triangle unit using a red 2½" square and a tan 2½" square. Press the seam allowance toward the red triangle. Make 96.

Make 96.

2. Sew half-square-triangle units from step 1 to opposite sides of a tan 2½" square as shown. Press the seam allowances toward the tan square. Make 24.

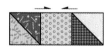

Make 24.

3. Sew tan 2½" squares to opposite sides of a half-square-triangle unit from step 1 as shown. Press the seam allowances toward the tan squares. Make 48.

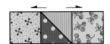

Make 48.

4. Sew together one unit from step 2 and two units from step 3 as shown. Press the seam allowances toward the step 2 unit. Make 24 A blocks.

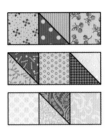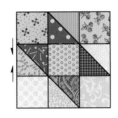

A block.
Make 24.

BLOCK B ASSEMBLY

1. Sew tan 2½" squares to opposite sides of a blue 2½" square. Press the seam allowances toward the blue square. Make 24.

Make 24.

2. Sew a blue 2½" square to a tan 2½" x 4½" rectangle as shown. Press the seam allowance toward the blue square. Make 48.

Make 48.

3. Sew together one unit from step 1 and two units from step 2 as shown. Press the seam allowances toward the step 1 unit. Make 24 B blocks.

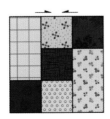

B block.
Make 24.

QUILT ASSEMBLY AND FINISHING

1. Arrange the blocks in eight rows of six blocks each, alternating the A and B blocks in each row and from row to row. Sew the blocks together in rows, pressing the seam allowances toward the B blocks. Sew the rows together. Press the seam allowances in the same direction.

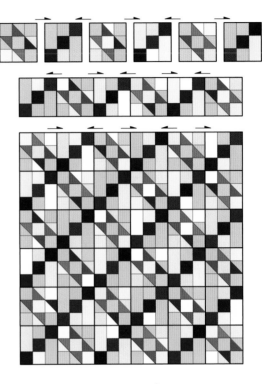

2. Referring to "Butted-Corner Borders" on page 12, add the red 2½"-wide inner-border strips and the tan 6"-wide outer-border strips.
3. Layer the quilt top, batting, and backing; baste the layers together. Quilt as desired.
4. Referring to "Binding" on page 15 and using the blue print 2½"-wide strips, bind the edges of the quilt.
5. Add a label.

Scrap-Basket Paddle Wheel

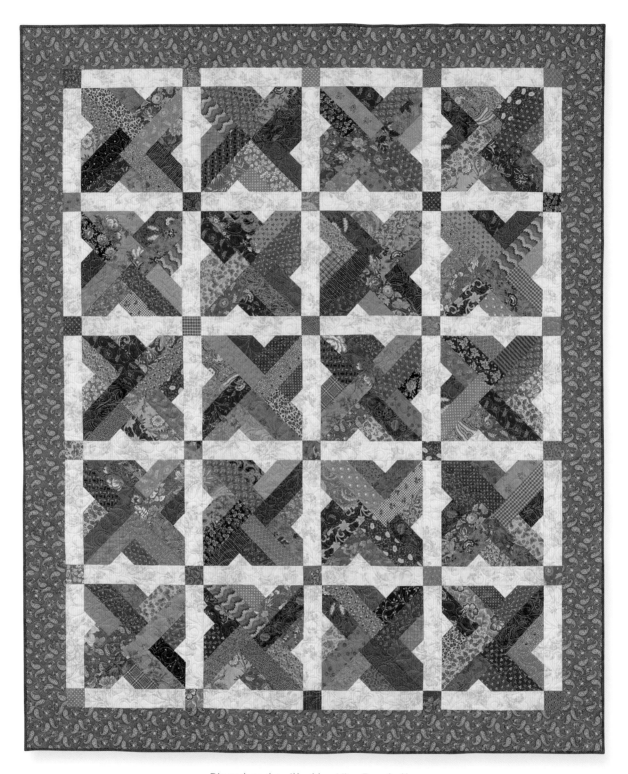

Pieced and quilted by Kim Brackett

This quilt couldn't be easier to piece, but you'll need to be mindful of the bias edges of the blocks. Handle them as little as possible until you add the sashing strips to each block.

FINISHED QUILT: 63½" x 76½" ❖ FINISHED BLOCK: 11" x 11"

MATERIALS

Yardages are based on 42"-wide fabric.

12 strips each, 2½" x 42", of assorted dark prints in reds, blues, browns, and greens for blocks and sashing posts (48 total)

1⅔ yards of light tan fabric for blocks and sashing strips

1⅛ yards of blue floral for border

⅔ yard of red print for binding

4¾ yards of fabric for backing

67½" x 80½" piece of batting

Square acrylic ruler, at least 12" x 12"

CUTTING

From each of 4 red, 4 blue, 4 brown, and 4 green strips, cut:

2 rectangles, 2½" x 8½" (32 total)

1 rectangle, 2½" x 6½" (16 total)

2 rectangles, 2½" x 4½" (32 total)

1 square, 2½" x 2½" (16 total)

From each of 4 different red, 4 different blue, 4 different brown, and 4 different green strips, cut:

2 rectangles, 2½" x 8½" (32 total)

2 rectangles, 2½" x 6½" (32 total)

1 rectangle, 2½" x 4½" (16 total)

From each of the remaining 4 red, 4 blue, 4 brown, and 4 green strips, cut:

1 rectangle, 2½" x 8½" (16 total)

2 rectangles, 2½" x 6½" (32 total)

2 rectangles, 2½" x 4½" (32 total)

1 square, 2½" x 2½" (16 total; you will have 2 left over)

From the light tan fabric, cut:

22 strips, 2½" x 42"; crosscut into:

49 strips, 2½" x 11½"

80 squares, 2½" x 2½"

From the blue floral, cut:

7 border strips, 5" x 42"

From the red print, cut:

8 binding strips, 2½" x 42"

CUTTING FROM SCRAPS

If you prefer to use scraps, follow the instructions below. See "Cutting" at left for instructions on cutting the border and binding.

From assorted dark prints, cut:

80 rectangles, 2½" x 8½"

80 rectangles, 2½" x 6½"

80 rectangles, 2½" x 4½"

30 squares, 2½" x 2½"

From assorted light prints, cut:

80 squares, 2½" x 2½"

49 rectangles, 2½" x 11½"

BLOCK ASSEMBLY

1. Sew a dark print 2½" x 4½" rectangle to a light tan 2½" square as shown. Press the seam allowance toward the dark rectangle. (Part of the rectangle will extend past the square. Don't worry about pressing this part—you'll trim it later.) Make 80.

Make 80.

2. Sew a dark print 2½" x 6½" rectangle to a unit from step 1 as shown. Press the seam allowance toward the newly added rectangle. Make 80.

Make 80.

3. Sew a dark print 2½" x 8½" rectangle to a unit from step 2 as shown. Press the seam allowance toward the newly added rectangle. Make 80.

Make 80.

4. Sew together four units from step 3 as shown. Press the seam allowances as shown. Make 20.

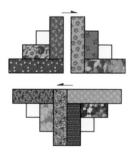

5. Square up each block to 11½". To do this, place the square ruler over a block so that the top and side edges align with the "V" that forms where the staggered strips meet, and the 45° line of the ruler is parallel to the center diagonal seam line. Trim off the top and sides. Rotate the block 180°, lining up the trimmed edges of the block with the 11½" markings on the ruler. Trim the top and right edges (above right). *All the block edges are now on the bias, so handle them carefully to avoid stretching them out of shape.*

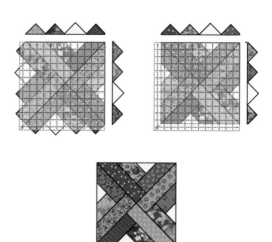

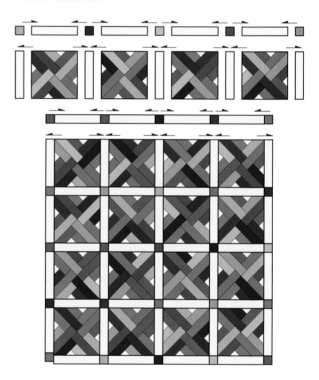

QUILT ASSEMBLY AND FINISHING

1. Arrange the blocks, the light tan 2½" x 11½" sashing strips, and the dark 2½" sashing posts as shown. Sew the pieces together in horizontal rows, pressing the seam allowances toward the sashing strips. Sew the rows together. Press the seam allowances in the same direction.

2. Referring to "Butted-Corner Borders" on page 12, add the blue floral 5"-wide border strips.
3. Layer the quilt top, batting, and backing; baste the layers together. Quilt as desired.
4. Referring to "Binding" on page 15 and using the red print 2½"-wide strips, bind the edges of the quilt.
5. Add a label.

Pieced and quilted by Kim Brackett

Use a variety of medium to dark batiks for this quilt to keep the design from getting lost. Carefully choosing and placing fabrics that contrast well with their neighbors will allow the "links" to appear as if they're woven together.

FINISHED QUILT: 53½" x 64¾" ❖ FINISHED BLOCK: 4" x 4"

MATERIALS

Yardages are based on 42"-wide fabric.

40 strips, at least 2½" x 30", of assorted medium to dark batiks for blocks

1⅓ yards of light batik for blocks and setting triangles

⅞ yard of brown batik for border

⅝ yard of multicolored batik for binding

3¾ yards of fabric for backing

57½" x 68¾" piece of batting

CUTTING

Before you begin cutting, lay out the 40 strips of medium to dark batik side by side, making sure that each fabric contrasts with the fabric next to it. Assign a placement order to the 40 fabrics using the assembly diagram on page 55 as a guide. You may find it helpful to label each strip with a numbered sticky note. As you cut the strips, keep the pieces together and in their placement order or numbered.

From each of the 40 assorted medium to dark batik strips, cut:

4 rectangles, 2½" x 4½" (160 total)

2 squares, 2½" x 2½" (80 total)

From the light batik, cut:

2 strips, 6⅞" x 42"; crosscut into 9 squares, 6⅞" x 6⅞". Cut each square twice diagonally to yield 36 quarter-square triangles.

3 strips, 4½" x 42"; crosscut into 22 squares, 4½" x 4½"

6 strips, 2½" x 42"; crosscut into 80 squares, 2½" x 2½"

From the brown batik, cut:

6 border strips, 4½" x 42"

From the multicolored batik, cut:

7 binding strips, 2½" x 42"

CUTTING FROM SCRAPS

If you prefer to use scraps, follow the instructions below, cutting the pieces in each set from the same fabric. See "Cutting" at left for instructions on cutting the border and binding.

From assorted dark prints, cut:

40 *sets of:*

4 rectangles, 2½" x 4½"

2 squares, 2½" x 2½"

From assorted light prints, cut:

9 squares, 6⅞" x 6⅞"; cut each square twice diagonally to yield 36 quarter-square triangles

22 squares, 4½" x 4½"

80 squares, 2½" x 2½"

BLOCK ASSEMBLY

To reduce bulk in the seam allowances, I suggest pressing the seam allowances of each block open.

1. Sew a medium to dark batik 2½" square to a light batik 2½" square. Press. Make two units from each of the 40 medium to dark batiks.

Make 2 from each fabric.

2. Sew a matching medium to dark batik 2½" x 4½" rectangle to the top of each unit from step 1. Press.

Make 2 from each fabric.

3. Sew together the remaining medium to dark batik 2½" x 4½" rectangles in pairs as follows: fabric 1 to fabric 2; fabric 2 to fabric 3; fabric 3 to fabric 4. Continue pairing up the rectangles in this manner through fabric 27. *Sew fabric 28 to fabric 1.* Beginning with fabric 29, sew fabric 29 to 30; fabric 30 to 31; fabric 31 to 32. Continue pairing up the rectangles in this manner through fabric 39. *Sew fabric 40 to fabric 29.* Press. Stack the rectangle units in the order sewn for ease in laying out your blocks.

QUILT ASSEMBLY AND FINISHING

1. Arrange the blocks from step 2 of "Block Assembly," the light batik 4½" squares, and the light batik setting triangles as shown.

2. Refer to the assembly diagram below to fill in the open areas with the corresponding rectangle units from step 3 of "Block Assembly."

3. Sew the blocks together in diagonal rows, continuing to press the seam allowances open. Sew the rows together. Press the seam allowances open.

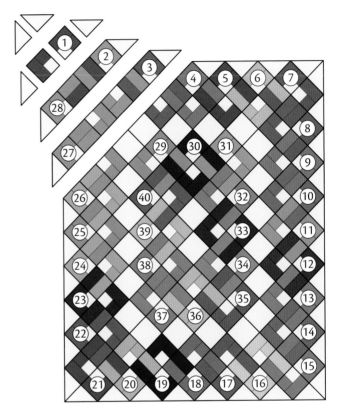

4. Referring to "Butted-Corner Borders" on page 12, add the brown batik 4½"-wide border strips. Press the seam allowances toward the border strips.

5. Layer the quilt top, batting, and backing; baste the layers together. Quilt as desired.

6. Referring to "Binding" on page 15 and using the multicolored batik 2½"-wide strips, bind the edges of the quilt.

7. Add a label.

Tipsy Baskets

Pieced and quilted by Kim Brackett

This quilt was made with lots of large-scale designer fabrics, including the one in the border that was pieced randomly without concern for where the motifs might appear. Just sew with abandon and let yourself be surprised.

FINISHED QUILT: 53½" x 61½" ❖ FINISHED BLOCK: 8" x 8"

MATERIALS

Yardages are based on 42"-wide fabric.

30 strips, 2½" x 42", of assorted light prints for blocks
20 strips, 2½" x 42", of assorted dark prints for blocks
1⅛ yards of large-scale red print for outer border
⅓ yard of blue print for inner border
⅝ yard of red print for binding
3¾ yards of fabric for backing
57½" x 65½" piece of batting

CUTTING

From *each* of the 30 assorted light print strips, cut:
2 rectangles, 2½" x 6½" (60 total)
7 squares, 2½" x 2½" (210 total)

From *each* of 10 assorted dark print strips, cut:
2 rectangles, 2½" x 6½" (20 total)
2 rectangles, 2½" x 4½" (20 total)
5 squares, 2½" x 2½" (50 total)

From *each* of the remaining 10 assorted dark print strips, cut:
1 rectangle, 2½" x 6½" (10 total)
1 rectangle, 2½" x 4½" (10 total)
7 squares, 2½" x 2½" (70 total)

From the blue print, cut:
5 border strips, 1½" x 42"

From the large-scale red print, cut:
6 border strips, 6" x 42"

From the red print, cut:
7 binding strips, 2½" x 42"

CUTTING FROM SCRAPS

If you prefer to use scraps, follow the instructions below, cutting the pieces in each set from the same fabric. See "Cutting" at left for instructions on cutting the borders and binding.

From assorted light prints, cut:
30 *sets* of:
    2 rectangles, 2½" x 6½"
    7 squares, 2½" x 2½"

From assorted dark prints for basket tops, cut:
30 *sets* of 3 squares, 2½" x 2½"

From assorted dark prints for basket bottoms, cut:
30 *sets* of:
    1 rectangle, 2½" x 6½"
    1 rectangle, 2½" x 4½"
    1 square, 2½" x 2½"

BLOCK ASSEMBLY

1. Select the squares and rectangles from one light print for the block background; three squares from one dark print for the basket top; and one 2½" x 6½" rectangle, one 2½" x 4½" rectangle, and one square from another dark print for the basket bottom.

2. Referring to "Folded-Corner Units" on page 17, make a half-square-triangle unit using one of the three matching dark print 2½" squares and a light print 2½" square. Press the seam allowance toward the dark triangle. Make three.

Make 3.

3. Sew together the half-square-triangle units from step 2 and a light print 2½" square as shown. Press the seam allowances as shown.

4. Make folded-corner units as shown using the matching dark print rectangles and light print 2½" squares. Press the seam allowances toward the light triangles.

5. Sew the folded-corner units from step 4 to the unit from step 3 as shown. Press the seam allowances toward the folded-corner units.

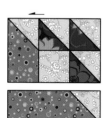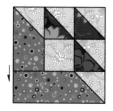

6. Sew a light print 2½" x 6½" rectangle to the unit from step 5 as shown. Press the seam allowance toward the rectangle.

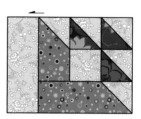

7. Make a half-square-triangle unit using the remaining dark print and light print 2½" squares.

Make 1.

8. Sew the half-square-triangle unit from step 7 to a light print 2½" x 6½" rectangle as shown. Press the seam allowance toward the rectangle.

9. Sew the unit from step 8 to the bottom of the unit from step 6. Press the seam allowance toward the unit from step 8.

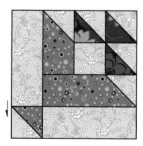

10. Repeat steps 1–9 to make a total of 30 blocks.

QUILT ASSEMBLY AND FINISHING

1. Arrange the blocks in six horizontal rows of five blocks each as shown, rotating every other block 180°. Sew the blocks together in rows, pressing the seam allowances in alternating directions from row to row. Sew the rows together. Press the seam allowances in the same direction.

2. Referring to "Butted-Corner Borders" on page 12, add the blue print 1½"-wide inner-border strips and the red print 6"-wide outer-border strips.
3. Layer the quilt top, batting, and backing; baste the layers together. Quilt as desired.
4. Referring to "Binding" on page 15 and using the red print 2½"-wide strips, bind the edges of the quilt.
5. Add a label.

Sparkler

Pieced and quilted by Kim Brackett

The pieced sashing strips in this quilt make the half-square-triangle units appear a little crooked. Use high-contrast fabrics for extra punch.

FINISHED QUILT: 59½" x 59½" ❖ FINISHED BLOCK: 6" x 6"

MATERIALS

Yardages are based on 42"-wide fabric.

32 strips, 2½" x 42", of assorted light cream prints for blocks, sashing strips, and sashing posts

21 strips, 2½" x 42", of assorted red prints for blocks and sashing strips

1⅛ yards of medium red print for outer border

⅓ yard of dark red print for inner border

⅝ yard of red floral for binding

4¼ yards of fabric for backing

63½" x 63½" piece of batting

CUTTING

From *each* of 24 assorted light cream strips, cut:

2 rectangles, 2½" x 4½" (48 total)

11 squares, 2½" x 2½" (264 total)

From *each* of the remaining 8 assorted light cream strips, cut:

1 rectangle, 2½" x 6½" (8 total)

1 rectangle, 2½" x 4½" (8 total; you will have 4 left over)

11 squares, 2½" x 2½" (88 total; you will have 3 left over)

From *each* of 17 assorted red strips, cut:

3 rectangles, 2½" x 4½" (51 total)

10 squares, 2½" x 2½" (170 total)

From *each* of the remaining 4 assorted red strips, cut:

1 rectangle, 2½" x 4½" (4 total; you will have 3 left over)

13 squares, 2½" x 2½" (52 total; you will have 6 left over)

From the dark red print, cut:

5 border strips, 1½" x 42"

From the medium red print, cut:

6 border strips, 6" x 42"

From the red floral, cut:

7 binding strips, 2½" x 42"

CUTTING FROM SCRAPS

If you prefer to use scraps, follow the instructions below. See "Cutting" at left for instructions on cutting the borders and binding.

From assorted red prints, cut:

216 squares, 2½" x 2½"

52 rectangles, 2½" x 4½"

From assorted light prints, cut:

349 squares, 2½" x 2½"

8 rectangles, 2½" x 6½"

52 rectangles, 2½" x 4½"

BLOCK ASSEMBLY

1. Referring to "Folded-Corner Units" on page 17, make a half-square-triangle unit as shown using a red 2½" square and a light cream 2½" square. Press the seam allowance toward the red triangle. Make 216.

Make 216.

2. Sew two half-square-triangle units from step 1 to opposite sides of a light cream 2½" square as shown. Press the seam allowances toward the cream square. Make 36.

Make 36.

3. Sew together two half-square-triangle units from step 1 and a light cream 2½" square as shown. Press the seam allowances as shown. Make 72.

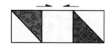

Make 72.

4. Sew together one unit from step 2 and two units from step 3 as shown. Press the seam allowances toward the units from step 2. Make 36 blocks.

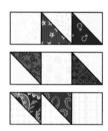 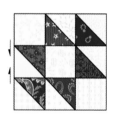

Make 36.

SASHING ASSEMBLY

Referring to "Split Units" on page 17, make a split unit using a red 2½" x 4½" rectangle and a light cream 2½" x 4½" rectangle. Press the seam allowance toward the red fabric. Make 52.

Make 52.

QUILT ASSEMBLY AND FINISHING

1. Arrange the blocks, pieced sashing units, cream 2½" x 6½" sashing rectangles, and cream 2½" sashing posts into horizontal rows as shown. Sew the pieces together in horizontal rows, pressing the seam allowances toward the sashing strips. Sew the rows together. Press the seam allowances in the same direction.

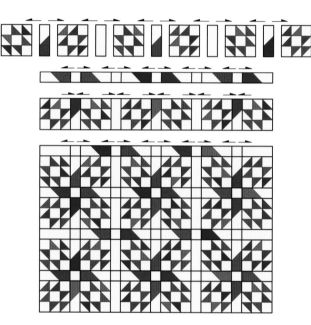

2. Referring to "Butted-Corner Borders" on page 12, add the dark red print 1½"-wide inner-border strips and the medium red print 6"-wide outer-border strips.
3. Layer the quilt top, batting, and backing; baste the layers together. Quilt as desired.
4. Referring to "Binding" on page 15 and using the red floral 2½"-wide strips, bind the edges of the quilt.
5. Add a label.

Pieced and quilted by Karen Williamson

The arrangement of this quilt center creates an illusion of layered blocks. If you aren't fond of pastel fabrics, use dark prints in place of the pastels, and a light background fabric in place of the dark brown.

FINISHED QUILT: 64½" x 64½" ❖ FINISHED BLOCK: 8" x 8"

MATERIALS

Yardages are based on 42"-wide fabric.
64 strips, at least 2½" x 35", of assorted pastel prints
    for blocks
2⅜ yards of brown marbled print for blocks and binding
4½ yards of fabric for backing
68½" x 68½" piece of batting

CUTTING

From each of the 64 pastel print strips, cut:
1 rectangle, 2½" x 8½" (64 total)
2 rectangles, 2½" x 6½" (128 total)
2 rectangles, 2½" x 4½" (128 total)
1 square, 2½" x 2½" (64 total)

From the brown marbled print, cut:
31 strips, 2½" x 42"; crosscut 24 strips into 384 squares,
    2½" x 2½". Set aside the remaining strips for the binding.

CUTTING FROM SCRAPS

If you prefer to use scraps, follow the instructions below. See "Cutting" above for instructions on cutting the binding.

From assorted pastel prints, cut:
64 rectangles, 2½" x 8½"
128 rectangles, 2½" x 6½"
128 rectangles, 2½" x 4½"
64 squares, 2½" x 2½"

From assorted dark brown prints, cut:
384 squares, 2½" x 2½"

BLOCK ASSEMBLY

1. Referring to "Folded-Corner Units" on page 17, make a half-square-triangle unit using a pastel print 2½" square and a brown marbled print 2½" square. Press the seam allowance toward the brown triangle. Make 64.

Make 64.

2. Sew a brown marbled print 2½" square to the light side of a half-square-triangle unit from step 1. Press the seam allowance toward the brown square. Make 64.

Make 64.

3. Make a folded-corner unit using a pastel print 2½" x 4½" rectangle and a brown marbled print 2½" square. Press the seam allowance toward the brown triangle. Make 128.

Make 128.

4. Sew together one unit from step 2 and two units from step 3 as shown. Press the seam allowances *open*. Make 64.

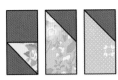 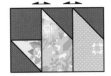

Make 64.

5. Make a double folded-corner unit as shown using a pastel print 2½" x 6½" rectangle and two brown marbled print 2½" squares. Press the seam allowances toward the brown triangles. Make 64.

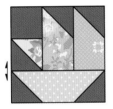

Make 64.

6. Sew a unit from step 5 to the bottom of a unit from step 4 as shown. Press the seam allowances *open*. Make 64.

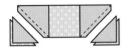

Make 64.

7. Sew a pastel print 2½" x 6½" rectangle to the top of a unit from step 6. Press the seam allowances *open*. Make 64.

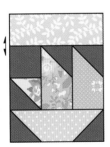

Make 64.

8. Sew a pastel print 2½" x 8½" rectangle to the side of the unit from step 7 as shown. Press the seam allowances *open*. Make 64 blocks.

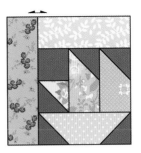

Make 64.

QUILT ASSEMBLY AND FINISHING

1. Arrange the blocks into eight horizontal rows of eight blocks each, rotating the blocks as shown to form the design. Sew the blocks together in rows, pressing the seam allowances open. Sew the rows together. Press the seam allowances *open*.

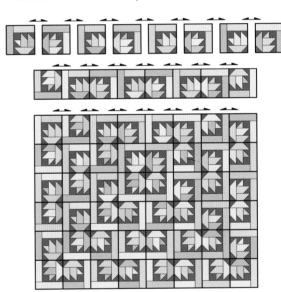

2. Layer the quilt top, batting, and backing; baste the layers together. Quilt as desired.
3. Referring to "Binding" on page 15 and using the seven remaining brown marbled print 2½" x 42" strips, bind the edges of the quilt.
4. Add a label.

Pieced and quilted by Kim Brackett

Use light and dark fabrics in any style or color for this easy-to-piece quilt. You'll be surprised by how quickly it goes together.

FINISHED QUILT: 48½" x 60½" ❖ FINISHED BLOCK: 6" x 6"

MATERIALS

Yardages are based on 42"-wide fabric.
35 strips, 2½" x 42", of assorted light batiks for blocks
26 strips, 2½" x 42", of assorted dark batiks for blocks
½ yard of multicolored batik for binding
3½ yards of fabric for backing
52½" x 64½" piece of batting

CUTTING

From *each* of 32 assorted light batik strips, cut:
3 rectangles, 2½" x 6½" (96 total)
4 rectangles, 2½" x 4½" (128 total)

From *each* of the remaining 3 assorted light batik strips, cut:
6 rectangles, 2½" x 6½" (18 total; you will have 2 left over)

From *each* of the 26 assorted dark batik strips, cut:
5 rectangles, 2½" x 4½" (130 total; you will have 2 left over)
5 squares, 2½" x 2½" (130 total; you will have 2 left over)

From the multicolored batik, cut:
6 binding strips, 2½" x 42"

CUTTING FROM SCRAPS

If you prefer to use scraps, follow the instructions below. See "Cutting" at left for instructions on cutting the binding.

From assorted light batiks, cut:
112 rectangles, 2½" x 6½"
128 rectangles, 2½" x 4½"

From assorted dark batiks, cut:
128 rectangles, 2½" x 4½"
128 squares, 2½" x 2½"

BLOCK ASSEMBLY

1. Referring to "Split Units" on page 17, make a split unit as shown using a dark batik 2½" x 4½" rectangle and a light batik 2½" x 4½" rectangle. Press the seam allowance toward the light fabric. Make 128.

Make 128.

2. Referring to "Folded-Corner Units" on page 17, make a folded-corner unit as shown using a light batik 2½" x 6½" rectangle and a dark batik 2½" square. Press the seam allowance toward the dark triangle. Make 32.

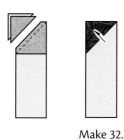

Make 32.

3. Make a double folded-corner unit as shown using a light batik 2½" x 6½" rectangle and two dark batik 2½" squares. Press the seam allowances toward the dark triangles. Make 48.

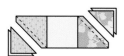

Make 48.

4. To make block A, sew together a light batik 2½" x 6½" rectangle, a folded-corner unit from step 2, and a split unit from step 1 as shown. Press the seam allowances toward the light rectangle. Make 32 blocks.

Block A.
Make 32.

5. To make block B, sew together two split units from step 1 and one double folded-corner unit from step 3 as shown. Press the seam allowances toward the double folded-corner unit. Make 48 blocks.

Block B.
Make 48.

QUILT ASSEMBLY AND FINISHING

1. Arrange the blocks in 10 horizontal rows of eight blocks each as shown, placing the A blocks around the outside edges and the B blocks in the center. Sew the blocks together in rows, pressing the seam allowances as shown. Sew the rows together. Press the seam allowances in the same direction.

2. Layer the quilt top, batting, and backing; baste the layers together. Quilt as desired.
3. Referring to "Binding" on page 15 and using the multicolored batik 2½"-wide strips, bind the edges of the quilt.
4. Add a label.

Pieced and quilted by Kim Brackett

Use contemporary prints for a quilt with a fun and fresh look, or choose another style or theme for a totally different effect. I'm itching to make this one with Christmas scraps!

FINISHED QUILT: 48½" x 60½" ❖ FINISHED BLOCK: 6" x 6"

MATERIALS

Yardages are based on 42"-wide fabric.
40 strips, 2½" x 42", of assorted dark prints for blocks
2 yards of light print for blocks
½ yard of multicolored print for binding
3½ yards of fabric for backing
52½" x 64½" piece of batting

CUTTING

From *each* of the 40 assorted dark strips, cut:
4 rectangles, 2½" x 6½" (160 total)
4 squares, 2½" x 2½" (160 total)

From the light print, cut:
25 strips, 2½" x 42"; crosscut into:
    80 rectangles, 2½" x 6½"
    160 squares, 2½" x 2½"

From the multicolored print, cut:
6 binding strips, 2½" x 42"

CUTTING FROM SCRAPS

If you prefer to use scraps, follow the instructions below, cutting the pieces in each set from the same fabric. See "Cutting" above for instructions on cutting the binding.

From assorted dark prints, cut:
80 *sets* of:
    2 rectangles, 2½" x 6½"
    2 squares, 2½" x 2½"

From assorted light prints, cut:
80 rectangles, 2½" x 6½"
160 squares, 2½" x 2½"

BLOCK ASSEMBLY

1. Referring to "Folded-Corner Units" on page 17, make a folded-corner unit as shown using a light 2½" x 6½" rectangle and two matching dark 2½" squares. Press the seam allowance toward the dark triangles. Make 80.

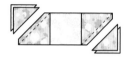

Make 80.

2. Make a folded-corner unit as shown using a dark 2½" x 6½" rectangle and a light 2½" square. Press the seam allowance toward the light triangle. Make 160 matching pairs.

Make 160.

3. Sew together one unit from step 1 and two matching units from step 2 as shown. Press the seam allowances toward the units from step 2. Make 80 blocks.

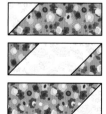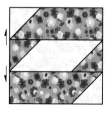

Make 80.

QUILT ASSEMBLY AND FINISHING

1. Arrange the blocks into 10 horizontal rows of eight blocks each, rotating the blocks as shown. Sew the blocks together in rows, pressing the seam allowances as shown. Sew the rows together. Press the seam allowances in the same direction.

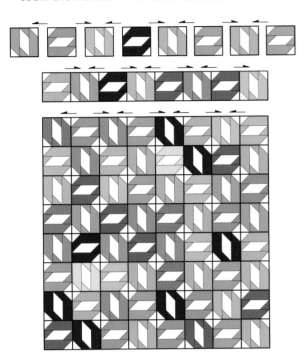

2. Layer the quilt top, batting, and backing; baste the layers together. Quilt as desired.
3. Referring to "Binding" on page 15 and using the multicolored print 2½"-wide strips, bind the edges of the quilt.
4. Add a label.

Northern Comfort

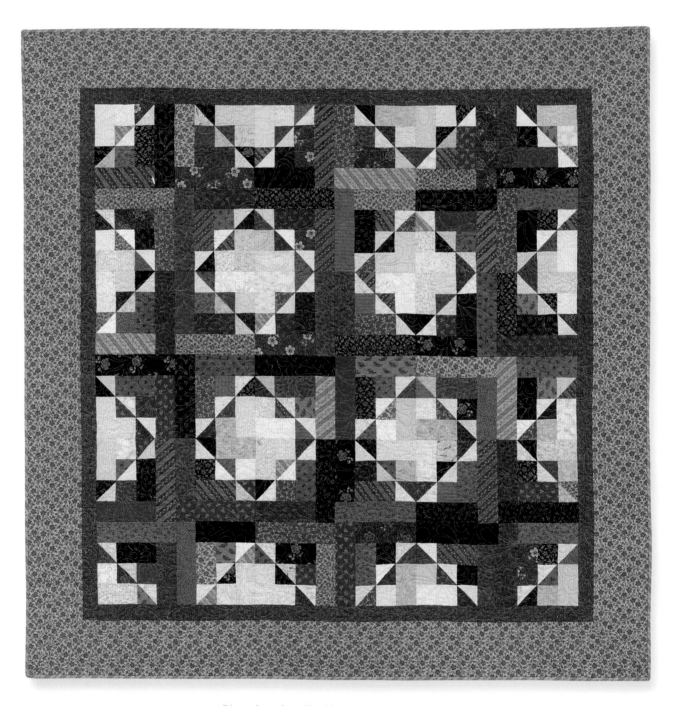

Pieced and quilted by Karen Williamson

I love the warm, rich colors Karen used in her quilt. For a totally different look, rotate the blocks in a diagonal "barn raising" setting.

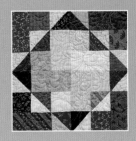

FINISHED QUILT: 62½" x 62½" ❖ FINISHED BLOCK: 8" x 8"

MATERIALS

Yardages are based on 42"-wide fabric.
29 strips, 2½" x 42", of assorted dark prints in blues,
   reds, browns, greens, and blacks for blocks
15 strips, 2½" x 42", of assorted light tan prints for blocks
1⅓ yards of red-and-tan print for outer border
½ yard of brown print for inner border
⅝ yard of tan striped fabric for binding
4¼ yards of fabric for backing
66½" x 66½" piece of batting

CUTTING

From *each* of 8 assorted dark print strips, cut:
2 rectangles, 2½" x 8½" (16 total; you will have
   1 left over)
1 rectangle, 2½" x 6½" (8 total)
1 rectangle, 2½" x 4½" (8 total)
4 squares, 2½" x 2½" (32 total)

From *each* of 7 different assorted dark print strips, cut:
1 rectangle, 2½" x 8½" (7 total)
2 rectangles, 2½" x 6½" (14 total)
1 rectangle, 2½" x 4½" (7 total)
5 squares, 2½" x 2½" (35 total)

From *each* of 7 different assorted dark print strips, cut:
1 rectangle, 2½" x 8½" (7 total)
1 rectangle, 2½" x 6½" (7 total)
2 rectangles, 2½" x 4½" (14 total)
5 squares, 2½" x 2½" (35 total)

From *each* of the remaining 7 assorted dark print strips, cut:
1 rectangle, 2½" x 8½" (7 total)
1 rectangle, 2½" x 6½" (7 total)
1 rectangle, 2½" x 4½" (7 total)
6 squares, 2½" x 2½" (42 total; you will have 6 left over)

From *each* of 8 assorted light tan strips, cut:
3 rectangles, 2½" x 4½" (24 total; you will have
   2 left over)
9 squares, 2½" x 2½" (72 total; you will have
   5 left over)

From *each* of the remaining 7 assorted light tan strips, cut:
2 rectangles, 2½" x 4½" (14 total)
11 squares, 2½" x 2½" (77 total)

From the brown print, cut:
6 border strips, 2" x 42"

From the red-and-tan print, cut:
7 border strips, 6" x 42"

From the tan striped fabric, cut:
7 binding strips, 2½" x 42"

CUTTING FROM SCRAPS

If you prefer to use scraps, follow the instructions below. See "Cutting" at left for instructions on cutting the borders and binding.

From assorted dark prints, cut:
36 rectangles, 2½" x 8½"
36 rectangles, 2½" x 6½"
36 rectangles, 2½" x 4½"
144 squares, 2½" x 2½"

From assorted light prints, cut:
36 rectangles, 2½" x 4½"
144 squares, 2½" x 2½"

BLOCK ASSEMBLY

1. Referring to "Folded-Corner Units" on page 17, make a half-square-triangle unit using one light tan 2½" square and a dark print 2½" square. Press the seam allowance toward the dark triangle. Make 108.

Make 108.

2. Sew a light tan 2½" square to the dark side of a half-square-triangle unit from step 1. Press the seam allowance toward the light tan square. Make 36.

Make 36.

3. Sew a light tan 2½" x 4½" rectangle to a unit from step 2. Press the seam allowance toward the light tan rectangle. Make 36.

Make 36.

4. Sew a dark print 2½" square to the light side of a half-square-triangle unit from step 1. Press the seam allowance toward the dark square. Make 36.

Make 36.

5. Sew a unit from step 4 to the bottom of a unit from step 3. Press the seam allowance toward the unit from step 3. Make 36.

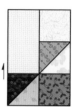

Make 36.

6. Sew a dark print 2½" x 4½" rectangle to the light side of a half-square-triangle unit from step 1 as shown. Press the seam allowance toward the dark rectangle. Make 36.

Make 36.

7. Sew a unit from step 6 to a unit from step 5. Press the seam allowance toward the unit from step 6. Make 36.

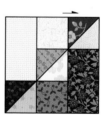

Make 36.

8. Sew a dark print 2½" x 6½" rectangle to the bottom of a unit from step 7. Press the seam allowances open. Make 36.

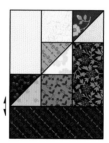

Make 36.

9. Sew a dark print 2½" x 8½" rectangle to the side of a unit from step 8. Press the seam allowances open. Make 36 blocks.

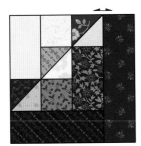

Make 36.

QUILT ASSEMBLY AND FINISHING

1. Arrange the blocks into six horizontal rows of six blocks each as shown. Sew the blocks together in rows, pressing the seam allowances as shown. Sew the rows together. Press the seam allowances in the same direction.

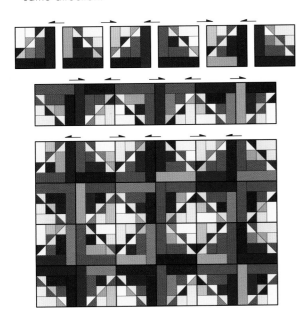

2. Referring to "Butted-Corner Borders" on page 12, add the brown print 2"-wide inner-border strips and the red-and-tan 6"-wide outer-border strips.
3. Layer the quilt top, batting, and backing; baste the layers together. Quilt as desired.
4. Referring to "Binding" on page 15 and using the tan striped 2½"-wide strips, bind the edges of the quilt.
5. Add a label.

Twinkle

Pieced and quilted by Kim Brackett

Substitute lime green or hot pink for the red prints in this quilt to make pinwheels with vivid personalities.

FINISHED QUILT: 49½" x 61½" ❖ FINISHED BLOCK: 6" x 6"

MATERIALS

Yardages are based on 42"-wide fabric.
24 strips, 2½" x 42", of assorted white-with-black prints for blocks
7 strips, 2½" x 42", of assorted red prints for blocks
1⅛ yards of red-black-and-white print for outer border
⅓ yard of red print for inner border
½ yard of black print for binding
3½ yards of fabric for backing
53½" x 65½" piece of batting

CUTTING

From each of the 7 assorted red strips, cut:
11 rectangles, 2½" x 3½" (77 total; you will have 5 left over)

From each of the 24 assorted white-with-black print strips, cut:
3 rectangles, 2½" x 6½" (72 total)
3 rectangles, 2½" x 5½" (72 total)

From the red print for inner border, cut:
5 strips, 1½" x 42"

From the red-black-and-white print, cut:
6 border strips, 6" x 42"

From the black print, cut:
6 binding strips, 2½" x 42"

CUTTING FROM SCRAPS

If you prefer to use scraps, follow the instructions below. See "Cutting" at left for instructions on cutting the borders and binding.

From assorted red prints, cut:
72 rectangles, 2½" x 3½"

From assorted white-with-black prints, cut:
72 rectangles, 2½" x 6½"
72 rectangles, 2½" x 5½"

BLOCK ASSEMBLY

1. Referring to "Split Units" on page 17, make a split unit as shown using a white-with-black print 2½" x 5½" rectangle and a red print 2½" x 3½" rectangle. Press the seam allowance toward the red fabric. Make 72.

Make 72.

2. To make block A, sew together two white-with-black print 2½" x 6½" rectangles and a split unit from step 1 as shown. Press the seam allowances as shown. Make 24 blocks.

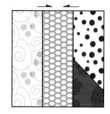

Block A.
Make 24.

3. To make block B, sew a split unit from step 1 to opposite sides of a white-with-black print 2½" x 6½" rectangle. Press the seam allowances as shown. Make 24 blocks.

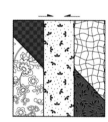

Block B.
Make 24.

QUILT ASSEMBLY AND FINISHING

1. Arrange the blocks in eight horizontal rows of six blocks each as shown. Sew the blocks together in rows, pressing the seam allowances as shown. Sew the rows together. Press the seam allowances in the same direction.

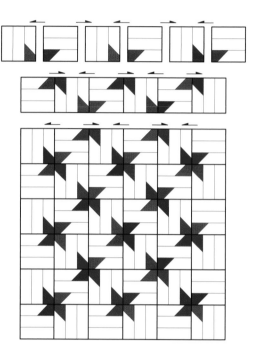

2. Referring to "Butted-Corner Borders" on page 12, add the red print 1½"-wide inner-border strips and the red-black-and-white print 6"-wide outer-border strips.

3. Layer the quilt top, batting, and backing; baste the layers together. Quilt as desired.

4. Referring to "Binding" on page 15 and using the black print 2½"-wide strips, bind the edges of the quilt.

5. Add a label.

About the Author

Kim Brackett lives in Gulf Breeze, Florida, with her husband and four cats. She works full-time as a paralegal in Pensacola and is a member of the Pensacola Quilters Guild.

Kim developed an interest in quilting in 1988 after admiring a collection of vintage quilts displayed in an antique shop. She began gathering tools, fabrics, and patterns, and finally finished her first quilt 10 years later in 1998! Although she prefers hand quilting, she has overcome many of the challenges of machine quilting and now enjoys finishing her quilts in much less time.

THERE'S MORE ONLINE!

Find out what's new with Kim by visiting her blog at www.magnoliabayquilts.blogspot.com.

This is Kim's second book about making quilts from 2½" strips. See the projects from her first book, *Scrap-Basket Surprises*, at www.martingale-pub.com.

You might also enjoy these other fine titles from

Martingale & Company

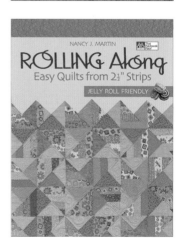

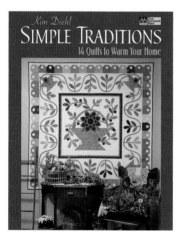

Our books are available at bookstores and your favorite craft, fabric, and yarn retailers.
Visit us at www.martingale-pub.com or contact us at:

1-800-426-3126
International: 1-425-483-3313
Fax: 1-425-486-7596
Email: info@martingale-pub.com

Martingale®
& C O M P A N Y

America's Best-Loved Craft & Hobby Books®
America's Best-Loved Knitting Books®

That Patchwork Place®

America's Best-Loved Quilt Books®